Florence
An architectural guide

itineraries
2

Guido Zucconi

Florence
An architectural guide

with an essay by
Pietro Ruschi

arsenale editrice

Guido Zucconi
FLORENCE
AN ARCHITECTURAL GUIDE

Design
Michela Scibilia

Translation
Antony Shugaar

Photographs
Michele Crosera

Photo credits
Biblioteca Medicea Laurenziana,
Florence (p. 15)
Gabinetto fotografico of the
Soprintendenza per i Beni
Ambientali e Architettonici of
Florence, Pistoia and Prato
(p. 13 and files no. 17, 18, 19,
21, 39, 46, 55, 59, 65, 82,
85, 89, 109, 111, 118, 121,
127, 142, 144, 145, 146, 157,
173, 180)

Printed in Italy by
EBS Editoriale Bortolazzi-Stei
Verona

First edition
may 1995

© Copyright 1995
Arsenale Editrice srl

*All rights reserved. No part of this
publication may be translated,
reproduced, stored in a retrieval system,
totally or partially adapted in any form
or by any means, microfilm,
photocopying or otherwise, without the
prior written consent of Arsenale
Editrice Venice. If granted, this
authorization is subject to the payment
of a royalty varying according to the
use intended for the publication.*

ISBN 88-7743-147-4

Contents

6   General plan

9   The architecture and the image of the city

23   Florence and Fiesole in the earliest times
27   Florence during the Romanesque Period
41   Florence during the Gothic Period
55   Florence during the time of Brunelleschi
77   Florence during the Cinquecento
97   Florence during the Seicento
109   Florence under the rule of the Lorraines
119   Florence during the Nineteenth and Twentieth Centuries
129   Florence and Modern Architecture

138   Glossary
140   Bibliography
141   Index of places
145   Index of names

QUARTIERE
SANTA MARIA NOVELLA

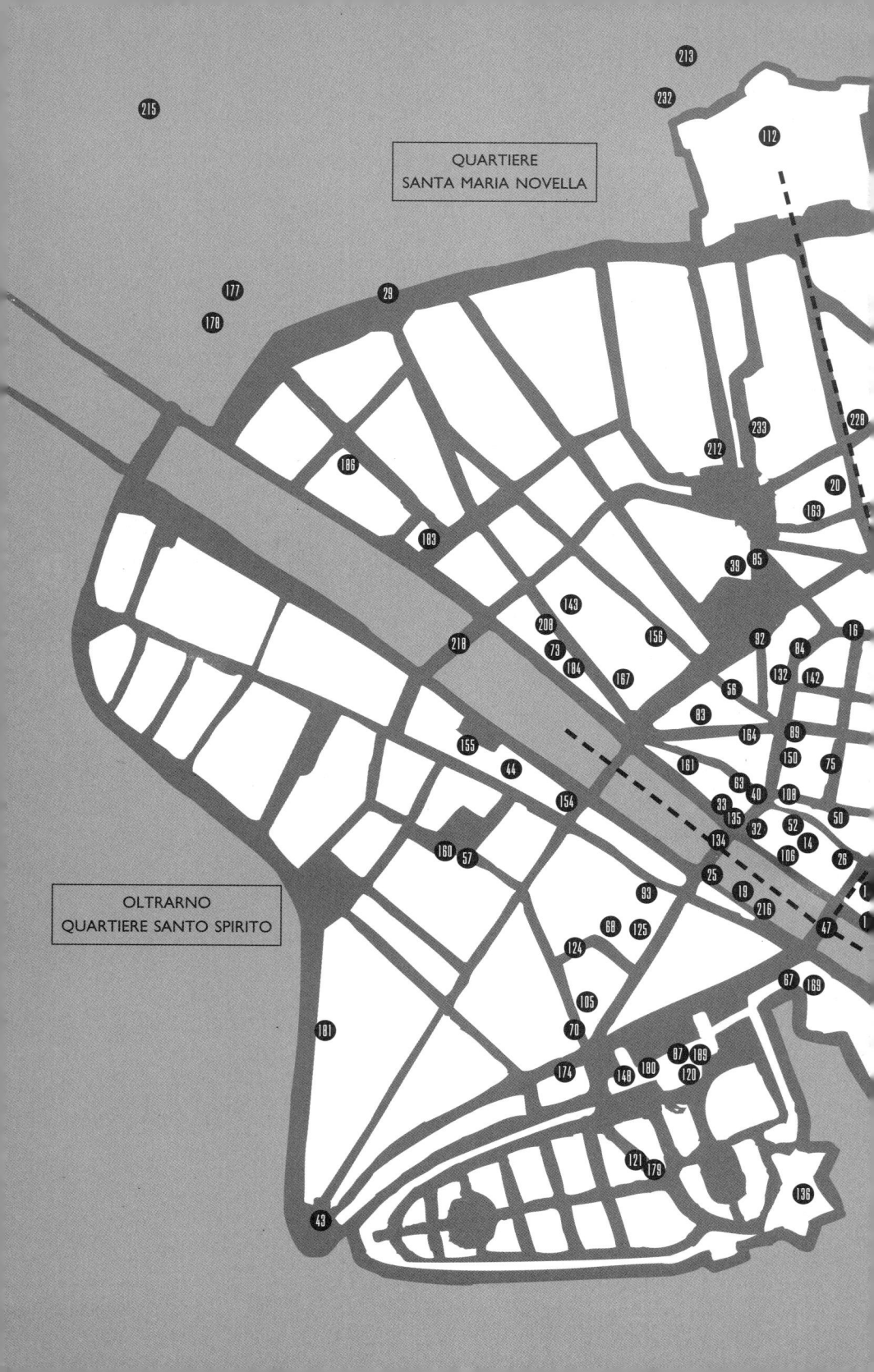

OLTRARNO
QUARTIERE SANTO SPIRITO

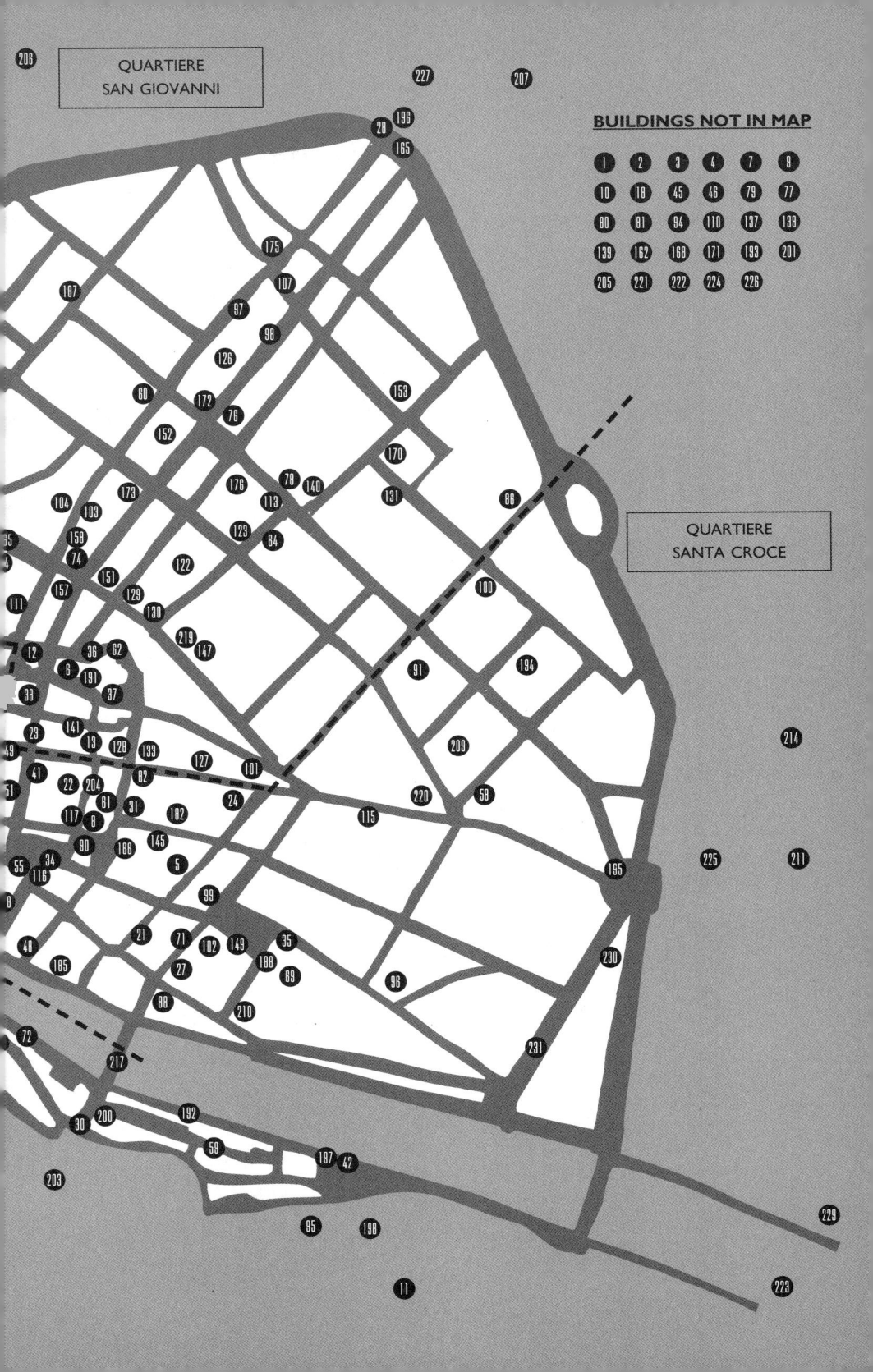

QUARTIERE
SAN GIOVANNI

QUARTIERE
SANTA CROCE

BUILDINGS NOT IN MAP

1 2 3 4 7 9
10 18 45 46 79 77
80 81 94 110 137 138
139 162 168 171 193 201
205 221 222 224 226

Sci Iois
batiste

Archiepi
scopat?

P. L cosme medias

Sca Laur.

Sca bernabe

D. petri fracia cōr
de medicis

Sn Dni bonifacij hosp.

SC

Pietro Ruschi

The architecture and the image of the city

Se dentro un mur, sotto un medesimo nome,
fusser raccolti i tuoi palazzi sparsi,
non ti sarian da pareggiar due Rome.
L. Ariosto, Le Rime

1
Pietro del Massaio, Iconographic Plan of Florence, around 1460. Detail of the Baptistery of San Giovanni and the Palazzo Medici, symbols of Florentine power and culture.

If one were to attempt to focus — through the imperfect lens of memory — on the image one has of Florence, it is almost certain that, in the wake of a solidly established mythology made up of unfading evocations that outshine even the remarkable creations of the Middle Ages, that image coincides with the city as it was during the Renaissance. And indeed the presence of buildings designed by Brunelleschi (ranging from the "structura sì grande, erta sopra e cieli" of the cathedral of Santa Maria del Fiore all the way to the "revolutionary" basilicas of San Lorenzo and Santo Spirito, to the palazzi and the churches, and on to the villas built by his followers – from Michelozzo and Benedetto da Maiano, to Giuliano da Sangallo and the Cronaca — this presence so deeply marked the city and the surrounding countryside that it somehow and irreversibly "froze" its image, greatly influencing the thoughts and tastes of the inhabitants, establishing a formal code that was to affect deeply virtually every building constructed ever since.

The model of the Renaissance, for artists and for historians, for the clients and for the Florentine people, became a constant point of reference in the building, modification, and expansion of the city, almost as if it had been a foreordained conclusion, so much so that there are attempts to see in the city's Romanesque and Gothic architecture preliminary indications of the direction that was later to be taken. Florentine Romanesque was strongly marked by elements of classical tradition, while the city's mature Gothic was distinguished by a solid, measured, severe character; and this was the world in which Brunelleschi worked and grew up. Thus, in Florence, the heritage of Brunelleschi's work permeates not only the architecture of the entire Quattrocento, but extends its influence well past the threshold of the following century, affecting and diluting the new ideas of the Baroque. This thread of continuity — after a brief and flimsy attempt at renewal in the mid-eighteenth century, prompted by the arrival of the Lorraine grand-dukes and, following them, by the French rule — carries through all the way to the second, more thorough "rinascita" (rebirth or renaissance, in Italian) of building, in the nineteenth century, culminating in Florence's brief period as capital of Italy, a time that sanctioned and established once and for all the "Renaissance" image of Florence (often in so doing, betraying the city's true nature, though never in the view of contemporaries, nor in the collective memory). It is therefore of little importance that the urban fabric presents a stratification that is variegated, and — especially for certain periods, in the wake of repeated restorations — of uncertain identification; it is of little importance that a careful analysis of the architecture of the fifteenth and sixteenth centuries shows that it is vastly outnumbered by buildings of the Middle Ages (during the thirteenth century, the population of Florence increased at least five-fold, expanding till it could rival the largest cities of Europe, with a consequential, enormous surge in construction) or those of the seventeenth and eighteenth centuries (the projects designed and built by someone like Gherardo Silvani or Antonio Ferri are far greater in number than those built by Brunelleschi), or especially those of the nineteenth century, which are found every-

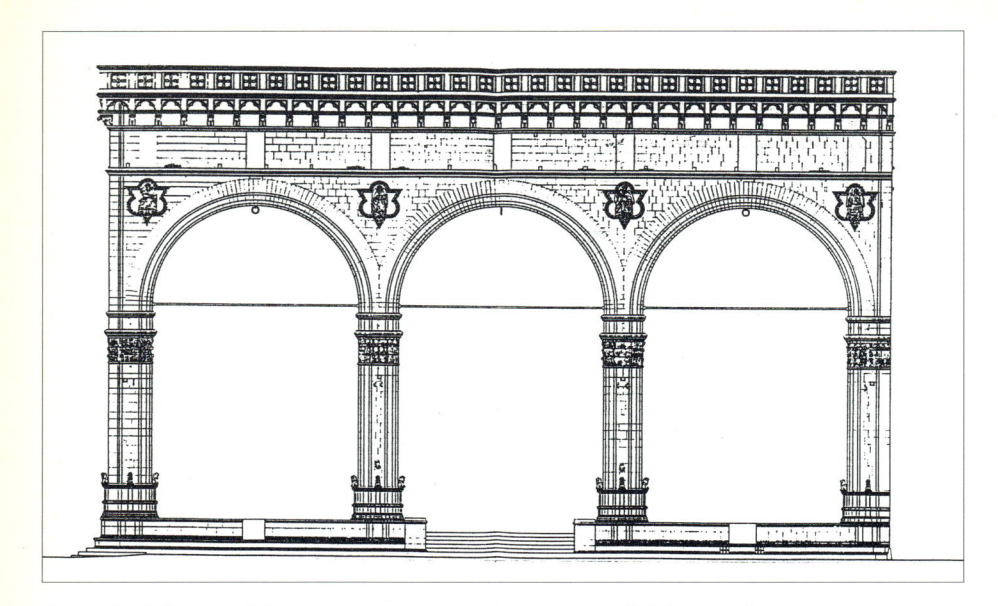

2
The Loggia della Signoria, built between 1374 and 1395, represents one of the highest expressions of the Florentine Gothic, in part due to its priceless array of sculpture (the marble *Virtues* and the stone heraldic devices).

3
The cathedral of Santa Maria del Fiore, from the church structure built by Arnolfo di Cambio to the cupola built by Brunelleschi, is certainly the greatest piece of architecture in the city, both in artistic and in technical terms.

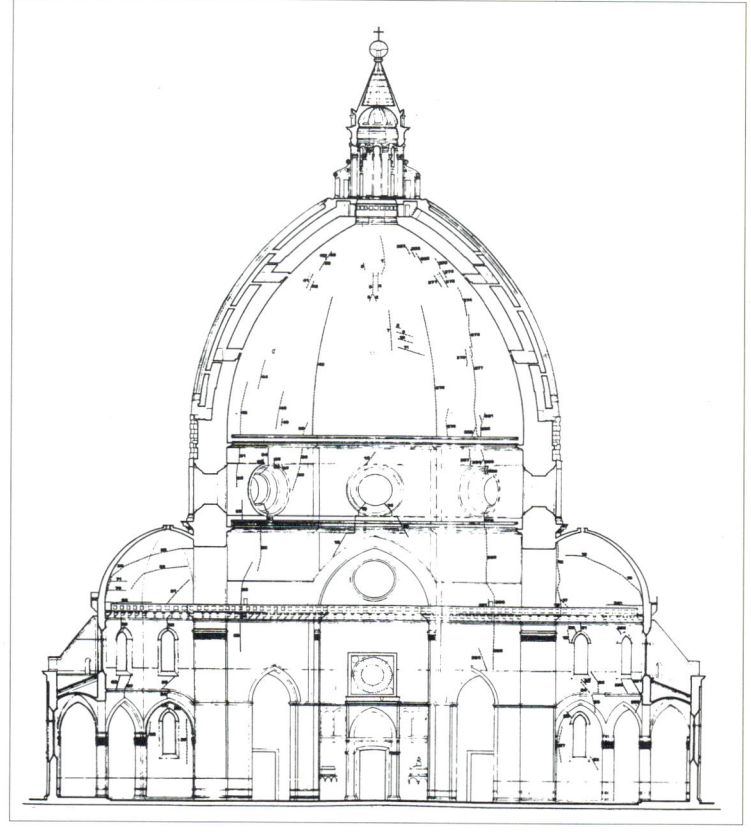

4
The basilica of San Lorenzo, which became the family church of the Medici, was rebuilt by Brunelleschi (and by those who continued his work), and then it received the great "additions" by Michelangelo (Biblioteca Medicea and Sagrestia Nuova), until the seventeenth century addition of the Chapel of the Princeps.

where, from the center to the outlying "Lungarni," all the way out to the hillside suburbs, built by Poggi following the destruction of the city walls. None of that matters very much: Florence always has been, and remains even now — in the eyes of one and all — the city of the Renaissance.

All of this, even if we remain in a strictly objective sphere, has its foundations and its explanations. The remarkable period of the Renaissance (especially the Renaissance tied to the first Medici "seigniory," from Cosimo, the *Pater Patriae*, to Lorenzo the Magnificent) constituted a decisive time of transition during which, because of political and economic events (in Florence and elsewhere), there was a consolidation of territorial power and a renewed vigor and development in the fields of philosophy, literature, and art (already quite vibrant in the late fourteenth century), bringing Florence to the threshold of complex mechanisms of formation and transformation of the remarkably hard-working and sophisticated social structure, that featured a dominant class (largely made up of an aristocracy of mercantile origins) that was culturally active and creative, with a major role in the Europe of the time, far greater than might have been expected from the city's relative political importance. This helped to cement in place that powerful civic sense — the so-called "Florentinism" — which was to be a constant of the city's culture and history. And it is certainly more than mere chance that the Roman origins of *Florentia* — adduced ever sice the communal era as a factor of legitimacy and of territorial and political autonomy ("libertas"), untiringly upheld with philological and esthetic arguments (such as those of Coluccio Salutati or Leonardo Bruni), and physically documented by the symbol of the city, the temple of Mars, which became the "bel San Giovanni" — that, as we were saying, those Roman origins should find their ultimate affirmation, in formal terms as well, in the art of the Renaissance, through the brilliant recovery and triumph on a European scale of the language of classical times: reinterpreted by Brunelleschi in a rational and modern context, conceptually "anti-classical" and then employed by many of Brunelleschi's followers in a far more literal fashion, with equal success.

Florence, then, as a "new Rome": this was a crucial concept for the Florentine culture of the Quattrocento, a "certainty" that is well expressed throughout the course of the city chronicles, as written by authors from Villani to Dei, a yearning toward a "mythical" supremacy that caught the imaginations of the city of as a whole, encouraging — especially in the second half of the century — a continuing surge in construction. "Et credo — wrote Giovanni Rucellai about his own money — che m'abbi facti più onore l'averli bene spesi ch'averli guadagnati e più chontentamento nel mio animo. E

[5] The Sagrestia Vecchia of San Lorenzo (1422-29) is the only building completed by Brunelleschi (along with the cupola of Santa Maria del Fiore). Because of the simultaneous presence of Donatello, it constitutes one of the most important — and intact — monuments of the entire Renaissance.

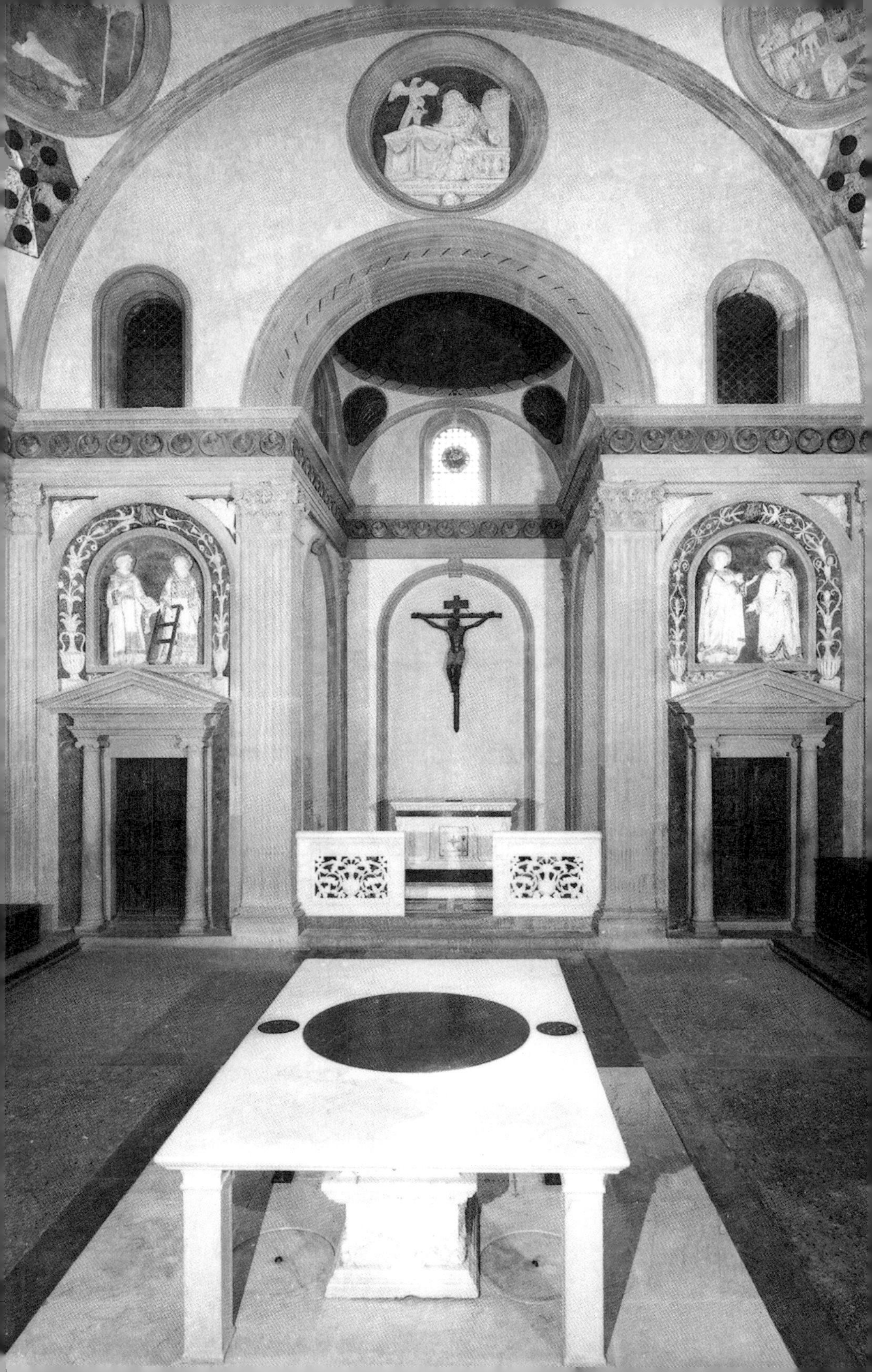

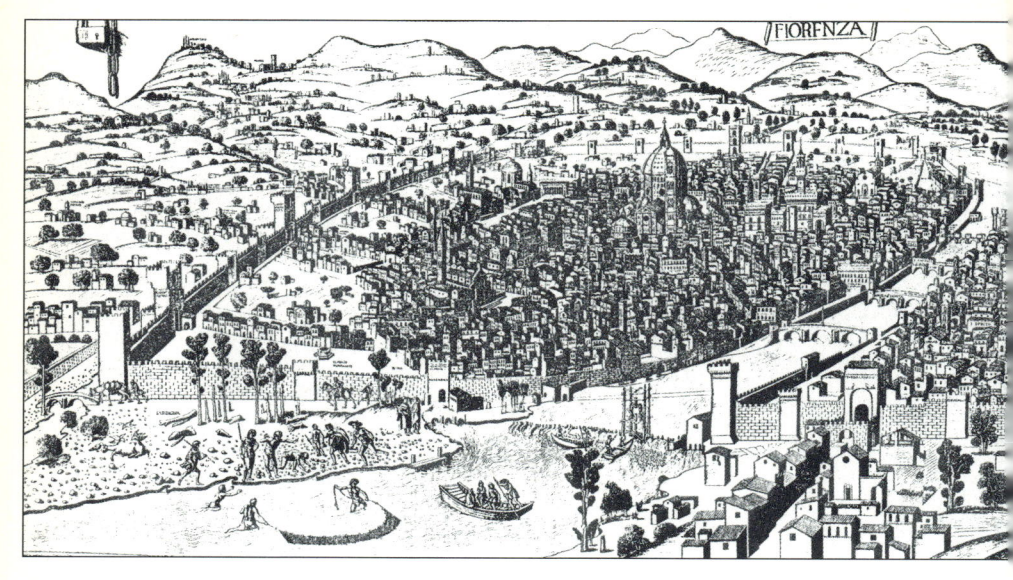

maximamente delle muraglie che io ò facte" — meaning, "And I believe that I have taken more honor from spending that money well, than from earning it in the first place, and that it created more contentment in my heart. And this is especially true of the walls that I have built."

The "bird's-eye view" of Florence, known as the "veduta della Catena," executed by Francesco Rosselli around the year 1472, shows the visible fruit of that century, set in the still intact fabric of the medieval "civitas," while showing as well the weighty and even burdensome heritage of that "glorious" image of the city of Lorenzo, a heritage from which it became difficult to escape: a model that had been attained, but which was thus no longer attainable.

As early as the beginning of the following century, at a time when the very conditions that had made Florence great and had put her at European center stage, were shifting, and in Rome's favor, it was possible to sense the weight of that inheritance, and it was only the presence of Leo X and Clement VII de' Medici on the papal throne that allowed a sort of shared artistic ideals and techniques to link the two cities, despite all of the political turbulence that separated them. (The work of Michelangelo is the most noble seal upon that bond). The Medici grand-dukes remained fundamentally loyal to that commonality, which was to bestow upon the Tuscan city the precious fruit of the late Renaissance, with the help of Vasari, Ammannati, and Buontalenti. And mistakenly Florence seems to have considered that fruit as a tangible continuation — and renewal — in the city under the grand dukes, of that mythical season in the past. In reality, the splendors of the late Renaissance were only the last few

6
Francesco di Lorenzo Rosselli, "Veduta della Catena" (about 1472-1480), Florence, Kunsthistorisches Institut. Florence is shown here with "scientific precision" by means of devices of perspective, at its point of maximum splendor, under the rule of Lorenzo the Magnificent.

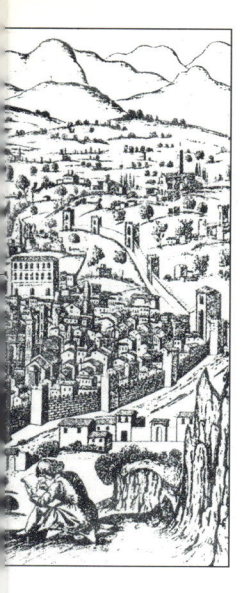

7
Attavante Attavanti, "La processione del Corpus Domini" ("The Procession of Corpus Domini," 1506), Florence, Biblioteca Medicea Laurenziana. This exquisite miniature offers a lively cross-section view of city life, as it shows the procession moving from the church of San Marco, and winding along the Via Larga in the direction of the cathedral.

anchors holding up a chapter that had actually long ended, and it was from that vantage point that henceforth Florence would look on passively at the development of Italian and European architecture. Following the numerous "croniche," or chronicles of the fourteenth and fifteenth centuries, including a few that were especially exacting in their descriptions of the city (Matteo Villani, Benedetto Dei, Goro Dati), there appeared as early as 1510 a book under the title *Memoriale di molte statue e pitture della Ciptà di Firenze* — *Account of Many Statues and Paintings of the City of Florence* — by Francesco Albertini; this work in many ways was a precursor of the countless "guides" to Florence, first and foremost among them, in 1591, the guide by Bocchi, expanded by Cinelli in 1677.

The "primacy" of the Renaissance emerges in all of the artistic and historiographic literature, especially from the second half of the eighteenth century, and then on for the rest of the following century,

8
The Palazzo Pandolfini, built to a plan by Raphael, in the early decades of the sixteenth century, provides documentation of the new Roman "manner" in Florence.

when the "success" of Florence, recognized as the second cradle of classicism, became universal, to the point of attracting — and influencing — a considerable portion of European culture. One sees the distant reflection of this phenomenon in the literature of the Romantics and in the more intelligent writers among the growing host of "literary voyagers" that were to visit Florence (from Goethe, Stendhal, and Madame de Staël to Viollet-le-Duc and Ruskin), as well as in the endless succession of "guidebooks" that were translated and printed in virtually every language: beginning with those by Cambiagi (first published in 1765, but followed by eleven separate editions, the last of them in 1819), and continuing with Gargiolli (1819), Ricci (1820), Marenigh (in French, 1822), François (1853), the Horners (printed in two volumes in London, in 1873), Burci (1875), and many many others too numerous to list here. From the end of the nineteenth century onward— let me mention only Burckhardt, Carocci, von Fabriczy, and Enlard — and especially beginning in the first decades of the twentieth century (let us mention only Davidsohn's monumental work on Medieval Florence, published in Berlin in 1908), there was a renewed philological exactitude that led to a new view of Florentine history, casting light on forgotten aspects and opening far-reaching debates on episodes that had been neglected till then.

Likewise, in the context of the history of architecture, a vast criti-

9
The great Baroque decorative structures, created to celebrate feasts and other special occasions, constitute a joyful but long-lost page of the city's history.

cal review of the facts was begun, both nationally and internationally; there was an effort to effectuate a new, "scientific" analysis of the countless pieces of evidence from the ancient past, but there were often also fluctuations of theory and esthetic, and in some cases, of ideology, that led to the favoring of certain periods. One instance of a case of this sort is that of Roman architecture and urbanism under the Fascist regime; another would be the interest — during the years immediately following the Second World War — in the Middle Ages and the Renaissance, to the complete exclusion of the Baroque (considered to be a "style-less" period), the eighteenth century, and even the nineteenth century. This slant on things led to devastating restorations and wrong-headed reconstructions. The consequences can still be felt in Florence: it continued through the Fifties and Sixties, and another major "revision," following the purist revision of the nineteenth century, swooped down upon many of the city's monuments.

This episode, like its counterpart of the nineteenth century, has remained artificially concealed, hidden beneath the intangible "Renaissance myth" of this city of art treasures, an aspect that is hardly glanced at even by the specialized literature, and certainly glossed over by the countless guidebooks, even the quite good ones, such as Grote (Munich, 1965), or Borsook (London, 1966). In these guidebooks, the section devoted to architecture is usually restricted to the more important buildings, because the topic was considered less appealing than the topics of painting and sculpture, which featured so many world-renowned works. It has not been until fairly recently that systematic, in-depth studies of the architectural heritage have begun, finally allowing us to consider each building in the context of the other buildings that surround it, and in the context of the ever-changing fabric of the city itself — one example of this sort of study is Giovanni Fanelli's "Firenze architettura e città," (Florence, 1973) and the exceedingly well documented volume by Richard A. Goldthwaite, *The Building of Renaissance Florence. An Economic and Social History* (Baltimora, 1980). The studies ranging all the way to the pitiless, but useful analysis of the actual results of more than a century of restorations of the best known monuments of Florence, M. Dezzi Bardeschi's *Il monumento e il suo doppio: Firenze* (exhibition catalogue, Florence 1981).

At the same time, a widespread effort at critical revision affected the general view, as well, of the so-called "minor" periods of Florentine architecture, leading finally to an adequate appreciation of some of the leading figures and creations of the period between the seventeenth and eighteenth centuries, with particular attention to the art of fresco-painting and plastic decoration that produced works of the first order in the churches and villas of the surrounding countryside. Finally, there was widespread recognition of the "technological" and environmental functions of the work of the neo-Classical period that had in many cases been hidden intentionally behind an inevitable neo-Renaissance veil; critics finally came to terms with the difficult-to-categorize period of nineteenth-century architecture, restoration, and urbanism, a phase that was inseparable from the work of Giuseppe Poggi — about whom monographs were written — and many other architects and engineers that had been virtually unknown until then. The architecture of the twentieth century, too, was the subject of considerable research. Through this reevaluation, there was renewed appreciation of the specific character and the importance of the work done in Florence, closely tied — in the more innovative work — to the activities of Giovanni Michelucci and the so-called "Tuscan Group," though there were also works that may have been a bit more traditional, but equally refined, by such architects as Raffaello Fagnoni and Angiolo Mazzoni.

Thanks to this revival of interest, which prompted numerous studies, conferences, and exhibitions, Florentine architecture, long thought to belong behind the much-lauded but, nevertheless, cast-iron "curtain" of the Middle Ages and the Renaissance, was finally seen in all its continuity, and public attention focused on that architecture, its functions, and its specific character. It has at last be-

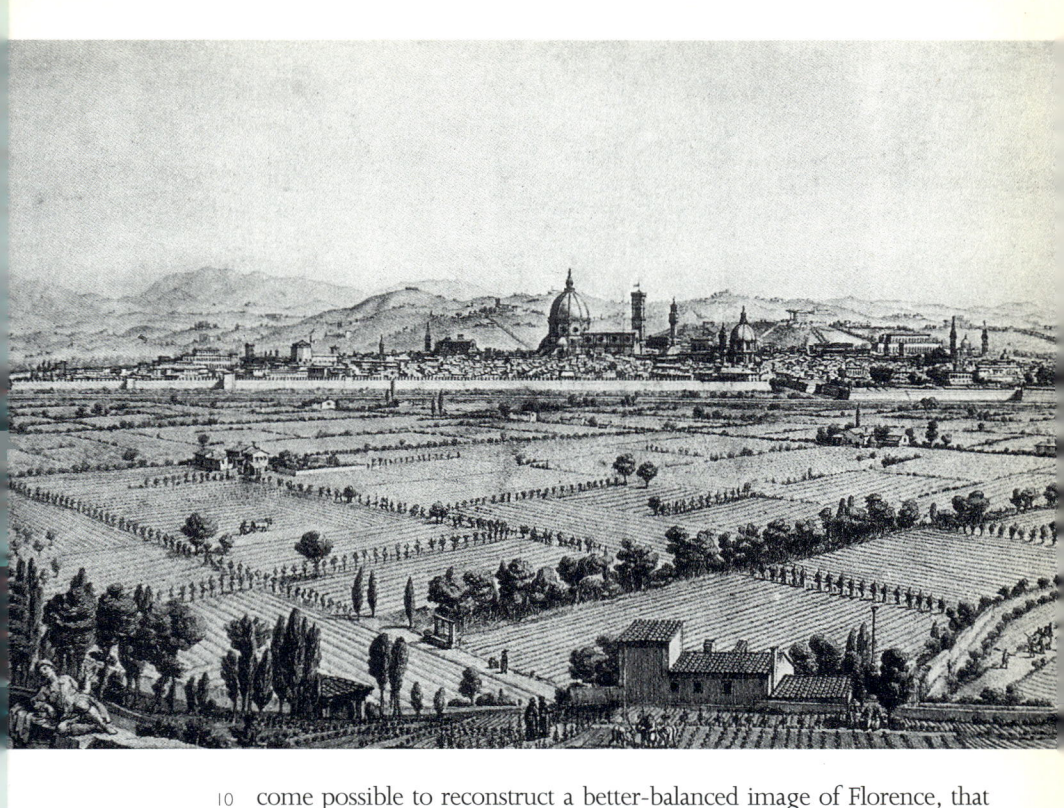

10 Giuseppe Zocchi, *View of Florence from the Convent of the Capuchin Fathers of Montughi*. This engraving, which forms part of the "Selection of XXIV Views" of Florence done in 1744 for the Marchese Gerini, testifies to the accuracy and thoroughness of description of the city and its setting that distinguished Florence's greatest view painter.

come possible to reconstruct a better-balanced image of Florence, that might better correspond to those cultural and social values that are certainly most directly expressed by architecture; this has in part been a result of a more accurate historical appreciation of the remarkable experience of the Renaissance, with an understanding of that experience in its true relationship to the architecture of later periods. And the fruit of that new appreciation, in terms of publishing, have been gathered in recent years: beginning with the great new appreciation for architecture that can be seen in Wigny's guidebook (D. Wigny, *Firenze*, published in Milan 1991) or in the updated, seventh edition of the guidebook *Firenze e dintorni*, by the Touring Club Italiano, one can then go on to consider the publication of specific architectural guides such as the large and well-researched guide put together by the Department of Architecture of the University of Florence (Turin 1992) or the other very recent guidebook by B. Giovannetti and R. Martucci, *Guida all'architettura di Firenze* (Venice 1994); and including the great and intriguing exhibition "Firenze e la sua immagine. Cinque secoli di vedutismo" (catalogue published in Venice 1994) that was held in the Forte Belvedere, and curated by the Assessorato alla Cultura, or Cultural Commission of the city of Florence.

The guidebook to Florentine architecture written and edited by Gui-

11
Lorenzo Gelati, *View of Florence from the Arno Upstream of the Bridge of San Niccolò* (1858-60), Florence, Collection of the Cassa di Risparmio di Firenze. Gelati painted one of the most "romantic" views of Florence, in perfect accord with the culture of his time.

do Zucconi fits into the context that we have attempted to set forth in this essay, to the point that it may be useful to set forth a number of considerations of those aspects that, in our opinion, most notably distinguish the work.

The remarkable conciseness of the files on each building — which fits in perfectly with the handy layout typical of a handbook — conceals a sort of "informational mechanism," in accordance with which two functions are served: on the one hand, brief but crucial information is provided concerning the building in question (architect or architects, chronology, location, photograph, and in many cases, floor plans), so as to satisfy the reader's immediate need to know; on the other hand, there are references, details, and other features that link the history of the individual to the larger issues of stylistic features, materials employed, techniques of construction, the relationship with the surrounding urban grid, so as to create an initial network of references, simple and very clear, capable of encouraging even those with no special knowledge of the topic to pursue other articles and books, turning to the essential but up-to-date bibliography found at the foot of each file. The efficacy of this approach is made even more valid by the considerable number of buildings treated, in the city and the surrounding areas, so as to constitute a very painstaking inventory, capable of surprising even the most inveterate connoisseurs of the architecture of Florence.

More than any aspect of the work of Guido Zucconi, however, we

12
Carlo Canella, *View of the Piazza della Signoria* (1847), Florence, Collection of the Cassa di Risparmio di Firenze. The critical monuments in the political history of fourteenth-century Florence, the Loggia della Signoria and the Palazzo Vecchio are depicted in the lively everyday life of a sunny afternoon in the mid-nineteenth century.

should focus on the very attitude, which at first sight might appear to be excessively rational and analytical, but which is actually the product of experience, a thorough knowledge, and correctness of approach. This attitude allows him to make an "impartial" observation of the city and its monuments, analyzing them with care but without undue emphasis, eluding — to the degree that this is possible — the snares and wiles of the great myths (foremost among them the Renaissance) without giving in to personal "inclinations" for any given period or style of architecture, limiting himself, quite simply, to providing information.

As a result, reading this guide may at first create the impression that everything is sailing by too quickly; after a little while, however, one soon detects, and comes to appreciate, the scientific rigor, the absence of clichés, the specific references, the intuitions, and the moderation of approach, the absence of prejudices, so that the reader is free to recall, to reason, to compare, and where it may seem appropriate, to venture into other readings. It is therefore quite clear that this guidebook is truly a "different sort" of tool, useful, pithy, efficacious, and eminently modern in terms of information. And in the end this little book truly becomes a sort of "toolbox, which offers with great clarity the instruments that are best suited for a sightseeing stroll and for a series of readings," as Donatella Calabi so accurately put it in the foreword to *Venice, an Architectural Guide*, also by Guido Zucconi.

QUARTIERE
SAN GIOVANNI

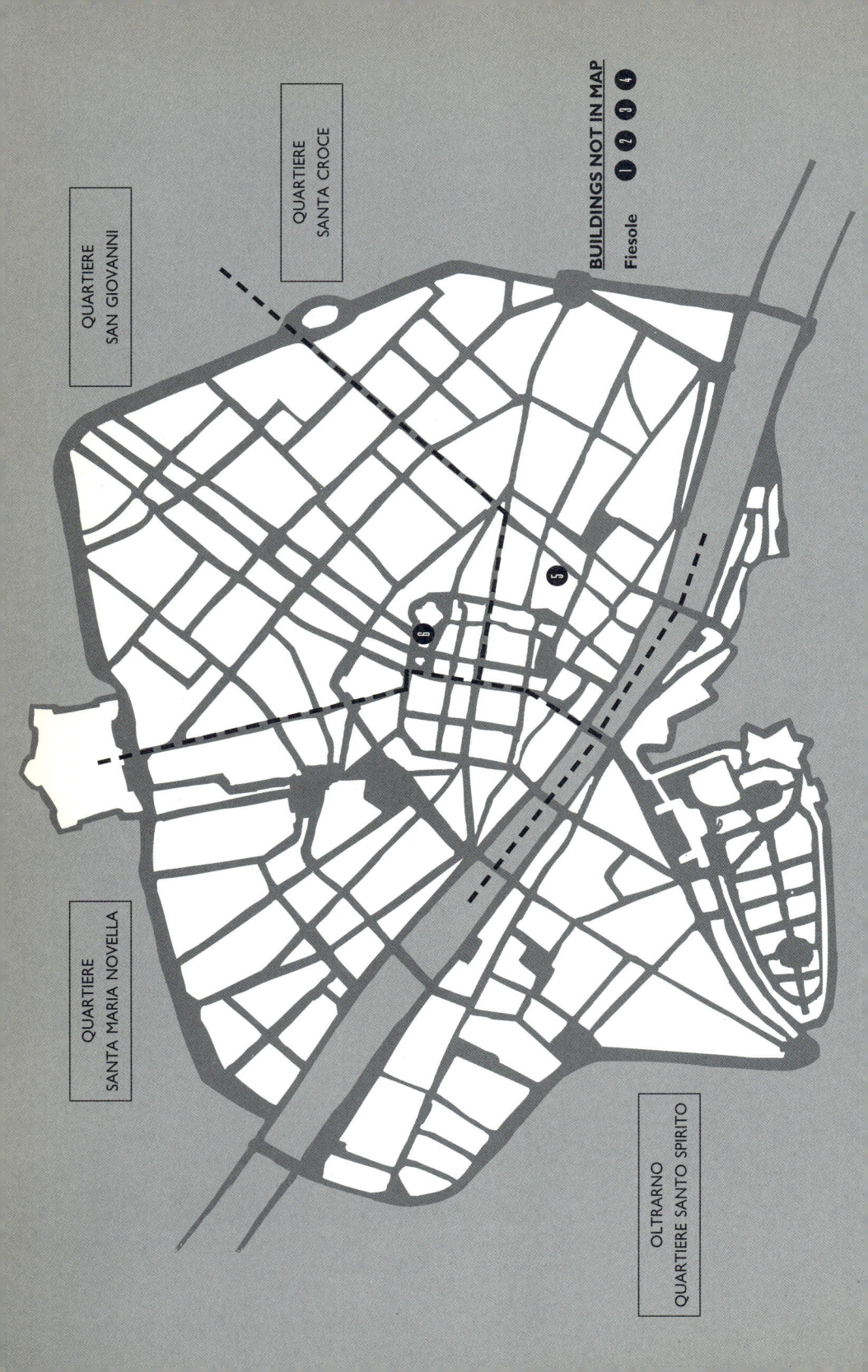

QUARTIERE
SANTA CROCE

QUARTIERE
SANTA MARIA NOVELLA

OLTRARNO
QUARTIERE SANTO SPIRITO

BUILDINGS NOT IN MAP
① ② ③ ④

Fiesole

Florence and Fiesole in the earliest times

Florentia was founded in 59 B.C. as a Roman *colonia*, in territory that had been completely and thoroughly organized along the regular grid of the *centuriae*; the advantages of this site clearly relate to the confluence of the river Mugnone and the Arno, with the Arno becoming navigable at precisely this point. Far more ancient is the Etruscan settlement of Fiesole, which may date from as early as the sixth or fifth century B.C.; in any case Fiesole is situated in a highly strategic location commanding the Arno valley. Urban life here, during Imperial times, was played out between the two structures of *Florentia* and *Faesulae*, between the *castrum* (or camp) in the plain and the *oppidum* (or fortress) on the hilltop, between the geometric city built to a grid, on the one hand, and the city that is organically implicit to the site, on the other. Originally, of far greater importance in political and demographic terms, the latter structure (modern-day Fiesole) still possesses a series of specific monuments (a theater, baths...). On the other hand, all that remains of the Florence of Roman times is the geometric grid of the urban layout; one can still see the *cardo* (running along Via Roma and Via Calimala) and the *decumanus maximus* (along the Via Strozzi and the Via del Corso). As early as the High Middle Ages, the roles of power had begun to shift and, well before the year 1000, Florence had become the chief city in the marquisate of Tuscany: the so-called *prima cerchia*, or earliest, eleventh-century inner circle of walls, enclosed an area far larger than the Florence of Roman times. While Fiesole dwindled into a hillside village, Florence grew, in size, and also in terms of economic and political power: by the end of the twelfth century, in the first glimmering dawn of the *secolo d'oro*, the city was unrivalled, not only in the Italian peninsula, but internationally as well.

Florence and Fiesole in the earliest times

1
Archeological area of Fiesole
3rd B.C.- 2nd century A.D.
Between the Via delle Mura Etrusche, Via Bandini and Via Dupré
Situated in the valley running between the hills of San Francesco and Sant'Apollinare, lies the area that was once the town's forum, where the most important public facilities were located: the baths, the theater, and the new temple. An element of continuity linking Etruscan and Roman eras, is the long stretch (about 250 meters) of town walls, built of sandstone blocks, along the north side of the area.

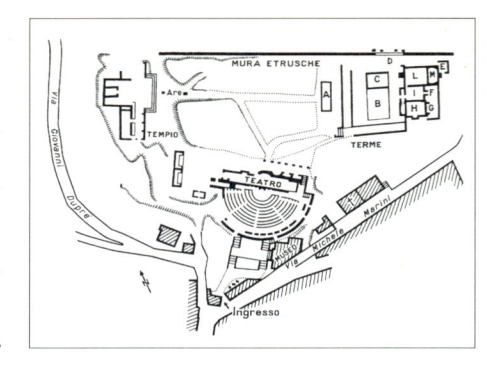

2
Ruins of the Temple of Fiesole
4th-1st century B.C.
Archeological area, Via Dupré
It was only at the turn of this century that this Etrusco-Roman complex was unearthed; here one can see the entrance stairway and a great deal of the enclosure wall; the older section lies in the central rectangle. During the time of the Roman Republic (first century B.C.), the temple was rebuilt and expanded, both in the wings and in the frontal section.

3
Theater of Fiesole
1st-2nd century A.D.
Archeological area, Via Dupré
This theater was first built in the earliest years of the Empire, and was subsequently renovated during the reign of Septimius Severus. The semicircular cavea (or tiered seating) has a diameter of 34 meters; the nineteen stepped tiers adhere to the natural slope, and are divided into four sectors, seating three thousand spectators. The scena and the orchestra are less well preserved.

4

Ruins of the Baths of Fiesole
1st-2nd century A.D.
Archeological area, Via Dupré
This structure was "discovered" in 1891; until that year, no one had guessed at the function served by the three arches, which had always been in full view. The remains of the three great swimming tanks, and the cryptoporticus around them, were finally identified as the three parts of the baths — the *calidarium*, *tepidarium*, and *frigidarium* — that were located somewhat to the east, and which been partly reconstructed following their excavation.

5

Traces of the Roman Amphitheater
2nd century A.D.
Quartiere Santa Croce, Piazza de' Peruzzi, Via Torta
The location, well beyond the easternmost limit of the *castrum*, coincides with the line of maximum expansion attained during Roman times. Today nothing survives but the elliptical shape (maximum diameter of 126 meters), which can be detected in the curving line of the building walls in the Via de' Bentaccordi, the Via Torta, and in the Piazza de' Peruzzi.

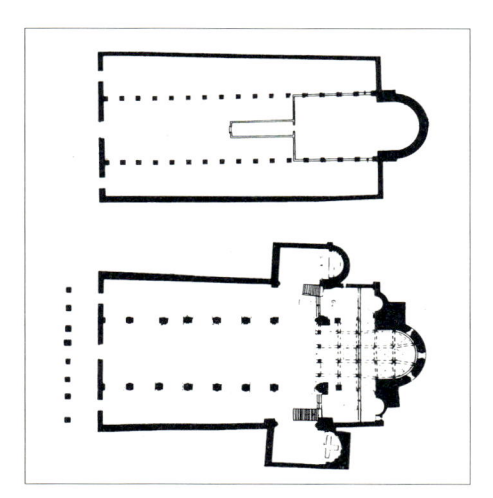

6

Ruins of the Church of Santa Reparata
4th-5th century A.D.
Quartiere San Giovanni, Piazza San Giovanni, (near the Cathedral)
By virtue of the excavations which were undertaken from 1966 to 1970, one can glimpse — beneath the floor of the Cathedral — a partial idea of the structure of the original metropolitan church, which was built on a basilican plan in early Christian times, later modified in the Middle Ages, and finally demolished in 1374. It has a nave and two side aisles and a raised choir, and is set within the first two bays of the Cathedral.

QUARTIERE SAN GIOVANNI

QUARTIERE SANTA CROCE

QUARTIERE SANTA MARIA NOVELLA

OLTRARNO
QUARTIERE SANTO SPIRITO

BUILDINGS NOT IN MAP
- Badia a Settimo — 7
- Fiesole — 9
- S. Domenico di Fiesole — 10
- Quartiere Campo di Marte — 18

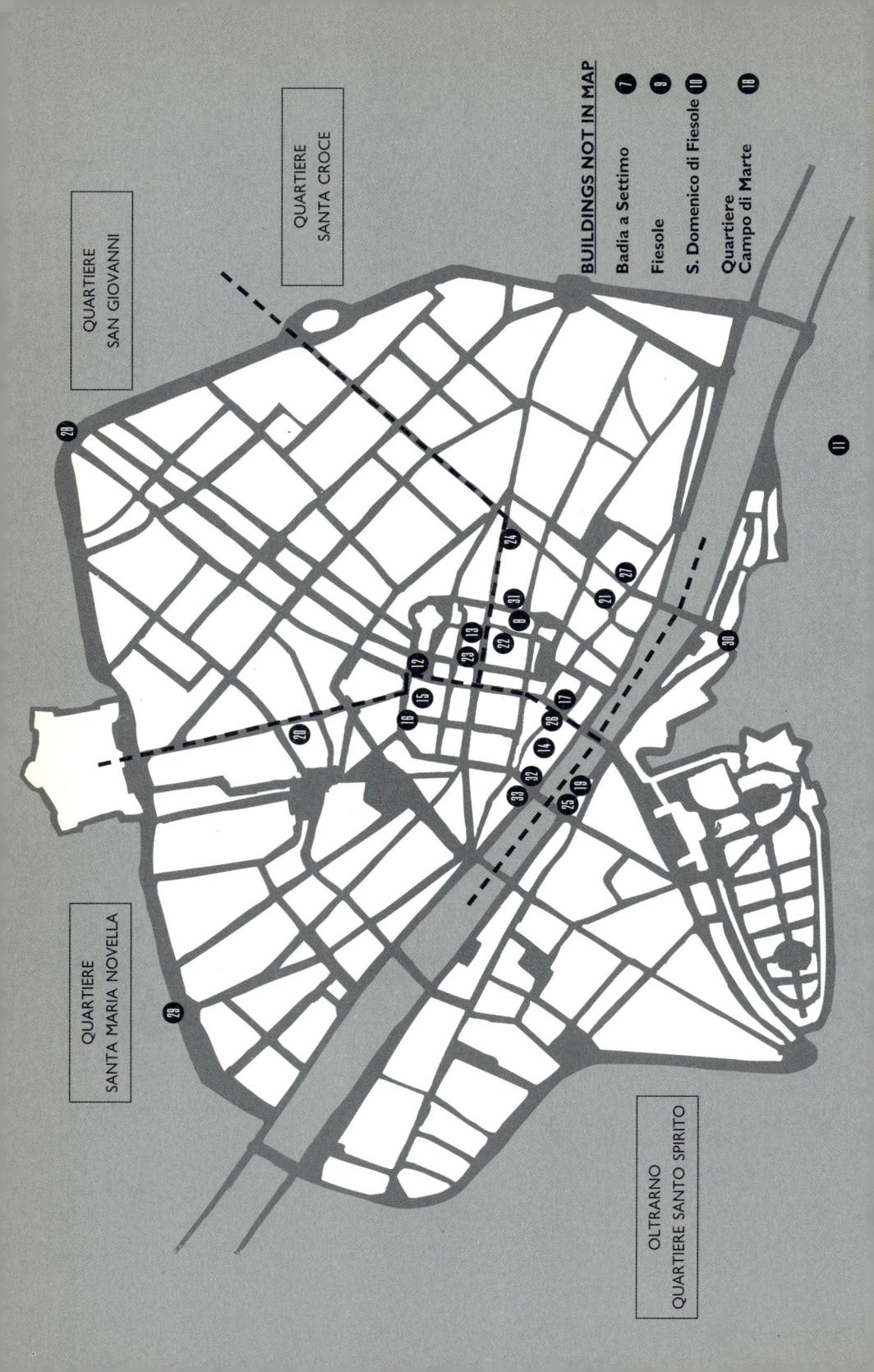

Florence during the Romanesque Period

The thirteenth century saw Florence at the height of its economic success: both history and lore reflect the supremacy of Florentine merchants in the markets of all Europe. Between the twelfth and thirteenth centuries, the city grew until it attained an unrivalled status in terms of size as well; in the city that produced Dante, however, the great material prosperity was not matched by a setting of corresponding political stability. During the "century of the Florentines," riven by the struggles among the various factions, the great wealth that the city had stored up did not yet produce architecture worthy of the city's wealth and status; "battlemented and iron-grey," thirteenth-century Florence proved to be split up amongst many factions, each of which rallied around the banner of one of the powerful clans, and the towers of their fortress-houses, which became the most distinctive features of the city. Outside of the city walls, at the crossroads of the major traffic arteries, conditions evolved for the establishment of major architectural complexes, built by various monastic orders. In the eleventh century, the Benedictines started building, followed in the thirteenth century by Franciscans and Dominicans, settling at opposite ends of the city and laying the groundwork for the two great projects of the fourteenth century: the churches of Santa Croce and Santa Maria Novella. It was not until the close of the century, however, following the triumph of the Guelph faction and the growing political power of the guilds, that it became possible to begin work on a number of major public works: the new city walls, the Palazzo dei Priori, and — most significant of all — the great church of Santa Maria del Fiore (Arnolfo di Cambio was the mastermind of this redoubled surge in construction).

Florence during the Romanesque Period

7

Abbey of San Salvatore
10th century and subsequent modifications
Badia a Settimo (near the exit of Signa, Autostrada del Sole), Scandicci
The modern-day appearance of a parish church on the outskirts of a city conceals what was, in the distant past, one of the most important Benedictine complexes in the Florence area, which developed in close correspondence to the burgeoning river traffic on the nearby Arno. The original structure can be detected in the façade and in the tripartite plan, much more than in the convent, which was expanded and transformed by the Cistercians during the thirteenth century.

8

Abbey of Florence
1282-1335
Arnolfo di Cambio and others
Quartiere Santa Croce, Via del Proconsolo
This church was founded by the Benedictines in the tenth century, near the eastern extremity of the city walls. It took on its current configuration, however, as it was reduced in size by a series of successive renovations. The first of these renovations is attributed to Arnolfo di Cambio, beginning in 1282: at that time, the interior space was reduced to a single nave, intersecting with ogival arches. In the new symmetrical plan, room was also made for the base of the bell tower, which had previously forced its way roughly into the original nave. Further restoration in the seventeenth century shifted the entrance (and with it, the main façade) by ninety degrees. The hexagonal bell-tower, built around 1330, is the best known feature, and has become one of the fundamental landmarks of the Florentine skyline. With its elongated biforate windows (or twin-light mullioned windows, hereinafter referred to by their Italian name, *bifore*), with its pointed spire, this tower possesses enormous upward thrust, and is traditionally attributed to Arnolfo di Cambio.

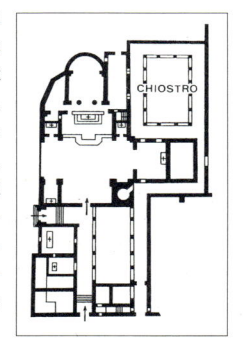

28

9
Cathedral of Fiesole
1024-28 and subsequent modifications
Piazza Mino da Fiesole

Built at the same time as the renovation of the Abbey (from which it took over as the episcopal church), this Romanesque building was enlarged in the thirteenth century, and further modified during modern times. The drastic nineteenth-century restoration emphasized its original plan with three aisles, with a transept, semicircular apse, and raised choir.

10
Abbey of Fiesole
1025-28 and subsequent modifications
San Domenico di Fiesole, Via di Badia

This church, and the convent of the Camaldolites, were founded in the High Middle Ages: the earliest rebuilding dates from the eleventh century; the second, most drastic reconstruction — which gave it its present appearance — dates from the fifteenth century (see no. 81). All that remains of the first reconstruction is a portion of the façade: this section appears today as a remarkable bit of polychrome structure, set in the bare surface of the great, unfinished façade. At the center of this finely poised piece of bicolored architecture appear three blind arches; together with the section above them, these arches are punctuated by geometric motifs that underscore their architectural layout, expressing an architectural syntax typical of the Florentine Romanesque, in accordance with a concept of surface treatment that we find once again in the Baptistery and in San Miniato.

11

San Miniato al Monte
1018-1207 and subsequent modifications
Oltrarno, Monte alle Croci

This is one of the most significant examples of polychrome Romanesque — whose allure is increased many-fold by the church's isolated location atop a hill overlooking the historical center of Florence. Successive renovations have done nothing to alter the basic nature of the church, constructed around the year 1000. The original character can be seen both in the unaltered marble decorations and in the bicolored geometric patterns, as well as in the plan; the three-nave construction is completed here with a raised choir, behind which rises the apsidal vault. The apparently homogeneous design of the church conceals the evidence of a lengthy process of construction that began with the decision of the bishop Hildebrand to rebuild the original church, which dated from the High Middle Ages (circa 1018); the conclusion of the process came in the early thirteenth century, when the distinctive triangle-shaped façade was completed. In its simplicity, the church is composed with a two-fold architectural order, and is covered with a bicolored marble surface, in accordance with a very precise geometric layout; here, as is the case in the Baptistery, as well, we see — in the lower section — a series of arches, some of them blind, and others open. In the upper section, the lesenes, or pilaster strips, create patterns and geometric spans that are emphasized by the constrasts of color; the same motifs appear in polychrome panels on the interior, punctuated by the arches that run along the perimeter. As further demonstration of an "antiquarian" style at work here, emphasizing the elements of continuity with the Greco-Roman culture, we find fragments of columns taken from classical structures, together with elements explicitly inspired by them.

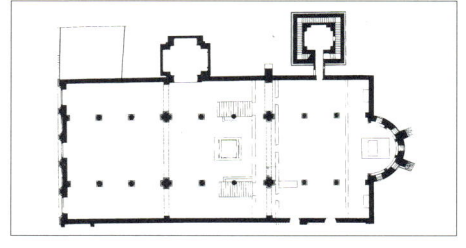

12
Baptistery of San Giovanni
11th-13th century and subsequent modifications
Quartiere San Giovanni, Piazza San Giovanni
Dedicated to Saint John, the patron saint of Florence, this building occupies a site used for various forms of worship ever since Roman times; little is known of its origins, save that they date from a period prior to the year 1000. It is no accident that the Baptistery became a building emblematic of medieval Florence, meant as an ideal, continuous link with classical antiquity. Until the year 1128 this had been the site of the cathedral, later moved to the site of Santa Reparata, the primary core of the future Cathedral of Santa Maria del Fiore.
The Baptistery is a structure with eight equal faces; in one of these eight faces, a rectangular body has been inserted. This great simplicity, as well as the surface treatment, with polychrome marble, complies with an overall geometric design, a two-dimensional mirroring of the architectural grid into which the octagon is subdivided. The decorative motifs are arranged in the spandrels and in the marble panels set in the triple arcades of each of the eight sides. The same motifs are also found in the upper fascia that joins the volume of the building with the cupola with triangular gores.
At the base of this "bicolored triumph of geometry" are set three bronze doors, two of which are the (renowned) work of Lorenzo Ghiberti. The tripartite organization reappears on the interior walls: in the upper fascia, the triple sets of *bifore* underscore the cavity, and hence the double dome that makes up the curtain wall.
This solution in all likelihood inspired Brunelleschi in his design for the cupola of the Cathedral.

13
Pagliazza Tower
6th and 11th-12th century
Quartiere San Giovanni, Piazza Santa Elisabetta 3
Evidence of this church's Byzantine origins can be seen in its circular plan, quite unusual in medieval Florence. After the year 1000, this tower was incorporated into the women's prison (which gave it its name); it then became the bell tower of the church of San Michele, since demolished. After 1970, it was "disencumbered" of the buildings that had concealed its lower section.

14
Church of the SS. Apostoli
10th-11th century and subsequent modifications
Quartiere Santa Maria Novella, Piazzetta del Limbo
Founded prior to the year 1000 as an extra-urban church, this building still conserves a few scattered original features (columns made of green marble, capitals) in the context of a still-basilican structure. In the center of the façade — drastically restored in the 1930s — stands the fifteenth-century portal.

15
Church of San Salvatore al Vescovo
11th century and subsequent modifications
Quartiere San Giovanni, Piazza dell'Olio
This church, adjacent to the Palazzo Vescovile, has been renovated several times since it was first built in the eleventh century. In the lower portion of the façade, the decorative pattern in bi-colored marble, completed in the thirteenth century, is particularly remarkable; with its effectively designed arches, it is reminiscent of the most significant examples of the genre (Baptistery, San Miniato).

16
Church of Santa Maria Maggiore
11th-13th century
Quartiere Santa Maria Novella, Via de' Vecchietti

Founded after the year 1000, this church is one of the oldest in Florence; its modern-day appearance, however, is a result of the rebuilding done during the second half of the thirteenth century. The façade and the sides are made of living stone, and have been extensively renovated. The interior, equally simple in basic conception, features three aisles with ogival arches and cross vaults.

17
Church of Santo Stefano al Ponte
11th-12th century and subsequent modifications
Quartiere Santa Croce, Piazza San Stefano

Of the original structure, nothing survives but part of the Romanesque façade, organized around the fourteenth-century portal made of polychrome marble. On the interior, only the rectangular shape of the external structure; a drastic renovation in the seventeenth century reduced its original Romanesque plan with three aisles into a single hall (see no. 146).

18
Church of San Michele a San Salvi
11th-16th century
Quartiere Campo di Marte, Piazza San Salvi

This church formed part of an abbey complex founded by the Order of the Vallombrosani in the eleventh century; partly destroyed during the siege of 1529, it was partly rebuilt in accordance with the original structure (though the portico on the façade clearly indicates its sixteenth-century style). The interior, with a single aisle, is built on a Latin-cross plan, with a rectangular apse, in accordance with the canons of monastic construction.

19
Church of San Jacopo sopr'Arno
12th century and subsequent modifications
Oltrarno, Borgo San Jacopo

Incorporated into the city's urban fabric, this Romanesque church features a three-arched portico dating from a later period, as do other parts of the building, which has been extensively modified: the restoration that followed the flood of 1966 led to the reclamation of many original features, such as the columns and the arches with fillets of bicolored marble.

20
Church of San Jacopo in Campo Corbolini
12th-13th century and subsequent modifications
Quartiere Santa Maria Novella, Via Faenza

In the unusual porticoed façade of this building, we find one of the few surviving instances of a medieval *atrium*; featuring semicircular arches set atop massive capitals, the façade has survived the subsequent renovations. Formerly a church of the Knights of Malta, the church has a fourteenth-century interior, and a single aisle split into two bays with a groin vault.

21
Church of San Remigio
13th-14th century
Quartiere Santa Croce, Via San Remigio

Founded after the year 1000, alongside a hospice for French pilgrims, the church was rebuilt in the late thirteenth century with extremely simple lines, with a triangle-shaped façade embellished by small hanging arches: on the interior, the early Gothic character can be seen in the ogival arcades that punctuate the three aisles, together with the octagonal pillars.

22

Castagna Tower
13th century
Quartiere Santa Croce, Piazza San Martino 1

This compact but slender structure was built to guard the Abbey, or Badia. Donated by the emperor to the monks, it was in turn given to the Commune of Florence, which designated it as headquarters for the Priori alle arti, before the completion of Palazzo Vecchio. Its non-partisan character saved it from the fate of the other towers, which were *scapitozzata* — to use the lively Florentine term for decapitation that was used to describe the process.

23

Tower-house of the Vedove (or of the Ghiberti)
13th century
Quartiere San Giovanni, Via del Corso 48 red

The unusual shape of an elongated parallelepiped leads one to think that here a number of buildings might have been incorporated. In the thirteenth century, this structure formed part of the defensive fortifications surrounding the vast portion of the city that was controlled, at the time, by the Adimari family. At the end of the fourteenth century, it was owned by Lorenzo Ghiberti (hence the family name, often used).

24

Tower-house of the Corbizi (or of the Donati)
13th century
Quartiere Santa Croce, Piazza San Pier Maggiore 35

This structure, particularly slender, rises in six different stories. The ground on which it stands was originally outside the city walls, and from here it commanded the village on the outskirts of town of the Albizi, a crucially strategic point guarding the road leading to Rome. It was a possession of the Guelph family of the Donati (hence the name, which is used alternatively).

25
Tower-house of the Marsili
13th century
Oltrarno, Borgo San Jacopo 7
Another tower which stood outside the penultimate set of city walls, it was built to defend the "alberghería" controlled by the Ghibelline family of the Ramaglianti. In comparison with other examples of the same genre, it shows a less haphazard arrangement of the architectural and decorative features, certain of which were clearly added in the nineteenth century.

26
Tower-house of the Amidei
13th century
Quartiere Santa Maria Novella, Via di Por Santa Maria 9, 11.
This building is also called "della Bigoncia," with a reference to the activity of dyeing practiced by the family that owned it. In the compact masonry one notices an uncommon array of openings, windows and doors, and decorative features, partly the result of radical restorations in the nineteenth century. Not all scholars agree, in this connection, whether the lion's heads, for which the tower is renowned, are authentic or not.

27
Tower-house of the Alberti
13th century
Quartiere Santa Croce, Via de' Benci, corner of Borgo Santa Croce
With its three fronts and with its pentagonal plan, this building adapts perfectly to the corner of the block on which it stands; for once, therefore, we see a tower that was not an attempt to force itself onto the surrounding context, but which harmonizes with its surroundings instead. At the base is an odd little fifteenth-century loggia with a canopy and slender little columns that are the namesakes of one of the oldest cafes in the city.

Florence during the Romanesque Period

28
Gate of San Gallo
1284
Quartiere Santa Maria Novella, Piazza della Libertà
This is one of the three city gates built in 1284, the first gates to be built in the new circuit of city walls on which work had just begun; here, more than elsewhere, one can clearly see the contrived nature of the urban planning that left the gate, isolated, in the center of a "piazza," completely uprooting it from its original context.

29
Gate of Prato
1284
Quartiere Santa Maria Novella, Viale Fratelli Rosselli
This is another of the first three gates to be built, as part of the defensive fortifications that were erected in the thirteenth century. Quite similar to Gate of San Gallo, it conserves the essential features common to this sort of structure: above the distinctive double-arched portal are trapdoors and loopholes that made it possible to check those entering and leaving and to defend the city.

30
Palazzo de' Mozzi
1260-73
Oltrarno, Via San Niccolò 123
In the last quarter of the thirteenth century, this building was considered to be the outstanding example of a "palazzo." In effect, it constitutes an early form of the Renaissance palazzo; however much it may have been renovated over the years, it offers a nice demonstration of the transition from the tower-house to the fourteenth-century model of house. To give an idea of its prestige, this palazzo was often used as a guest residence for prominent visitors, such as pope Gregory X and the duke of Athens.

31
Il Bargello (or Palazzo del Popolo)
Ca. 1256-1327, 1345-50
Neri di Fioravante, Benci di Cione
Quartiere Santa Croce, Via del Proconsolo

This building is traditionally considered to be the greatest achievement of the civil architecture of the thirteenth century, even though it is actually a blend of features dating from both the thirteenth and fourteenth centuries.

Designed as the headquarters of all of the institutions of the Comune (the "Palazzo del Popolo," or Palace of the People), it later became the headquarters of the "Podestà," or Mayor, with which it is still associated, even nowadays. From the sixteenth century onward it contained the headquarters of the "Bargello," or chief of police, and executions were held here. The adjectives "grim" and "iron-grey" have been used repeatedly in desciptions of this building, designed as a vast cubic mass, set alongside the existing Volognana Tower, a graceful but monolithic vertical structure. Built in regular blocks of stone, the thirteenth-century structure rises to the second string-course; above that line is the part that was added following the great fire of 1323, including the crowning structure, with the battlements and brackets to support a balcony.

The plan of the building revolves around a courtyard with an exterior staircase leading up to the upper floors, in accordance with the style found in merchants' homes of the thirteenth century. The only openings to be found in the compact interior façades are the portico on the ground floor and the loggia on the first floor. Here, in the structural features and the decorative motifs of the fourteenth century, we begin to see a distinctive character that clearly foreshadows the *esprit* of the following century; consider, for example, the cross-vaults which are supported by an alternation of pillars and corbels, in accordance with a module that was later developed by Brunelleschi in the "Ospedale degli Innocenti," or Foundling Hospital.

In 1865, it was set aside as a national museum, with a collection devoted chiefly to sculpture.

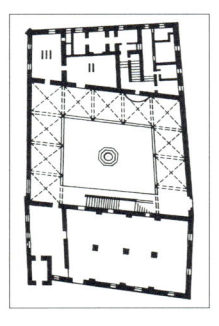

Florence during the Romanesque Period

32
Palazzo Feroni-Spini
Beginning in 1289
Quartiere Santa Maria Novella, Piazza Santa Trinita, corner of Borgo Santi Apostoli

The compact mass of this building, made out of living stone, is crowned with a complete circuit of jutting battlements; this motif, which we find in the Bargello, as well, in all likelihood served as the inspiration for the design of the Palazzo Vecchio, which was built only a few years later. With its façade rising three stories high, punctuated by windows with basket handle arches, this palazzo set the standard as it emerged in the years straddling the thirteenth and fourteenth centuries: it had no towers nor any particular vertical structures, and it rose to an even and uniform height, as was set forth in the new regulations governing private construction. Between 1861 and 1871 it was the headquarters of the City Government; later, a thorough-going restoration emphasized to an extreme degree the building's medieval aspects, with the removal of features that had been added subsequently, and isolating its great bulk from the architectural fabric of the city. At the same time, shops were allowed to set up in serried ranks, and they still occupy the ground floor today.

33
Palazzo Gianfigliazzi
Ca. 1290
Quartiere Santa Maria Novella, Piazza Santa Trinita 1

The façade of this building, too, reflects the building regulations established at the end of the thirteenth century. It formed part of one of the most important architectural features in late thirteenth-century Florence, together with Palazzo Frescobaldi (located on the far side of the Arno) and with Palazzo Feroni-Spini, located directly facing it: it features the same module of façade, culminating in a crowning battlemented walkway.

QUARTIERE SAN GIOVANNI

QUARTIERE SANTA CROCE

QUARTIERE SANTA MARIA NOVELLA

OLTRARNO
QUARTIERE SANTO SPIRITO

BUILDINGS NOT IN MAP

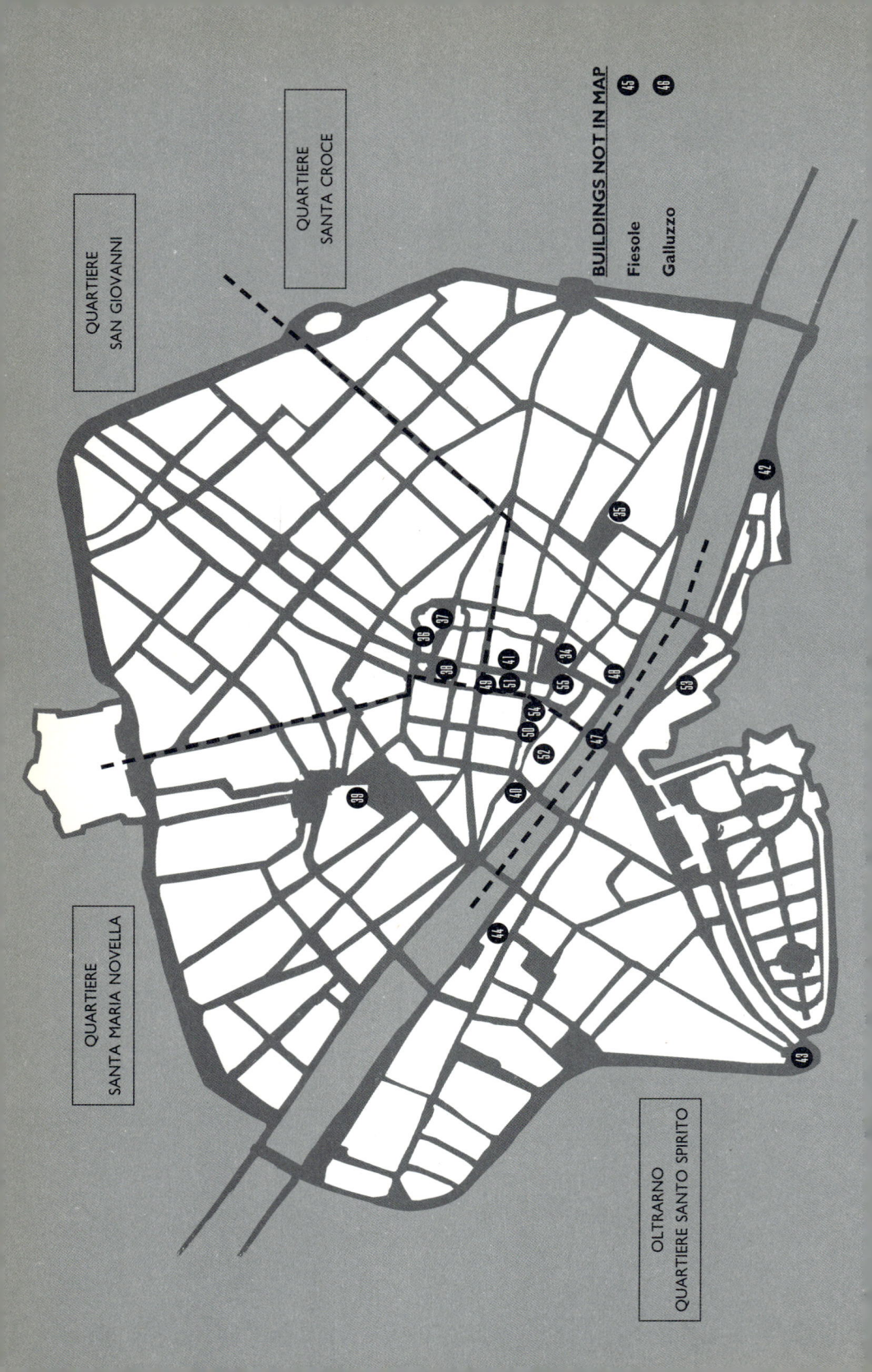

45 Fiesole
46 Galluzzo

Florence during the Gothic Period

Arnolfo di Cambio is considered to be the mastermind behind the works in this period that constitute — in their size and vertical thrust alone — radical breaks with the past. Two buildings, along with the newly built circuit of city walls, constitute the core of this new approach: the Palazzo dei Priori and the church of Santa Croce. The first of these two buildings was the headquarters and focal point of the city's public life, while the second was the chief city church. Both buildings reflect the pride of a city well aware of its position of economic and cultural leadership. Together with the churches of Santa Maria Novella and Santa Trinita, the building of Santa Croce forms part of a system that was just then being consolidated, a system of strategic strongpoints of the city. The plans for expansion of all three churches had been drawn up and work had begun during the thirteenth century, and work was completed during the fourteenth century. The construction went on in what amounted to ateliers, where the building art of the Cistercians, imported from the other side of the Alps during the twelfth and thirteenth centuries, was developed into new forms that led to the concept of the "Italian Gothic." The fact remains that, no matter how one may choose to interpret them, these projects were forerunners — in terms of architectural techniques and solutions — of the greatest architectural project of fourteenth-century Florence: the cathedral of Santa Maria del Fiore. In the city that gave the world Petrarch, Boccaccio, and Giotto, the construction of the cathedral lay the groundwork for the remarkable flourishing of the arts that was to characterize the Quattrocento, or fifteenth century; the cathedral, indeed, was to be the theater in which the opening acts would be performed of a revolution whose starring actor was to be Brunelleschi.

34

Palazzo Vecchio (or Palazzo dei Priori)
1299-1314
Arnolfo di Cambio
Quartiere Santa Croce, Piazza della Signoria
This building constitutes the greatest piece of civil architecture in Florence during the rule of the Comune; over time, with a view to an idea of continuity with the Middle Ages, it rose to become a symbol of the city itself. In reality, this building is the expression of a specific historical period, and in particular the new order of things brought about by the institutional reforms of 1298 (which came under the heading of the "Ordinamenti di giustizia") : the building was initially designed as the headquarters of the Priori delle Arti (whence the original name of the Palazzo dei Priori). A sort of "poetics of contrasts" distinguished its appearance, especially in the part that overlooks the piazza which was created especially for the occasion, through the demolition of the houses of a defeated family, the degli Uberti. The two-light mullioned windows, jutting elegantly and arranged in regular sequences, break up the uniform rustication of the volume; the crowning battlements emphasizes the building's fortress-like character, imparting greater solidity to the already massive structure of the lower body of the building. The building is given great upward thrust by the great belltower, called Arnolfo's Tower which was completed about 1310: this belltower replaced the previous de' Foraboschi Tower, whose base is incorporated in the shaft. The tower is crowned by a jutting walkway in all ways similar to that of the main building. The plan of the fourteenth-century building is organized around a pentagonal courtyard, in compliance with a model that had already been tested in the Bargello; on the interior, a great many changes were made during renovations in the fifteenth and sixteenth centuries, when the building was probably also enlarged toward the Via dei Leoni (see no. 116).

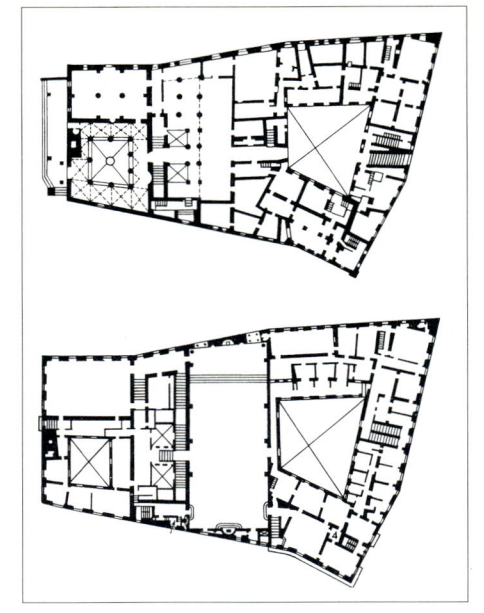

35

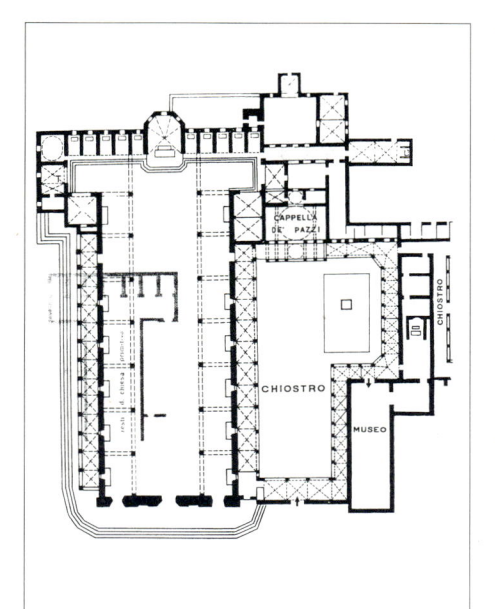

Church and Convent of Santa Croce
Beginning in 1294
Arnolfo di Cambio and others
Quartiere Santa Croce, Piazza Santa Croce

The building as it appears now was rebuilt, beginning in 1294, under the supervision of Arnolfo di Cambio, and it stands with the other great building projects of the turn of the century. At the end of the thirteenth century, the construction of the new city walls changed its status: from without the walls, it was suddenly within them; for the Franciscan community, this fact was crucial, and may have triggered the rebuilding process that continued until the late fifteenth century (the well known cycle of frescoes by Giotto date from about 1320).

The definitive layout of this church appears arranged according to a plan based on an Egyptian cross: the main part of the building is split up into a navem tzo aisles and eight bays, the last of which spreads crosswise until it takes on the function and size of a transept.

Remarkable in terms of conceptual simplicity and logical construction, the interior structure seems to mark a decisive watershed in the development of forms of an *autochthonous Gothic*, according to the opinions of a number of critics (see *Romanini 1969*).

In reality, however, the criterion of construction does not vary greatly from the vaulting systems used in other structures built around the same time, such as the Cathedral, Santa Trinita... A series of octagonal pilasters support ogival arches which, alternating with lesenes, punctuate the central nave, and correspond to the large transverse arches of the aisles.

The idea of establishing this as a sort of pantheon, at first for Tuscany, and with the passage of time, for all of Italy, dates from the period of the Medici, but it developed during the eighteenth and nineteenth centuries (the façade and the bell tower date from that period: see no. 188)

36
Cathedral (or Church of Santa Maria del Fiore)
1296-1421
Arnolfo di Cambio and others
Quartiere San Giovanni, Piazza del Duomo

In the initial phase of the construction of this building — traditionally believed to have been the work of Arnolfo di Cambio - the idea was that it somehow ran parallel to the construction of Palazzo Vecchio, constituting a sort of religious counterpart. The way in which construction continued, however, was quite different. Unlike the Palazzo Pubblico, the colossal scale of the construction of Santa Maria del Fiore was to require nearly a century-and-a-half of concerted effort by the city of Florence. The process culminated in the enormous undertaking of the cupola, during the Renaissance, or if one considers the façade to be the last step, during the nineteenth century (see no. 62, and no. 191).

The plan, which is quite atypical of the buildings of the fourteenth century, seems to highlight the difficulties of execution: it is the product of the joining of two distinct systems, one of which refers to the longitudinal body of the building, the other to the transept and to the apsidal section, and together they constitute an autonomous sector, conceived in accordance with a central plan. At the center is the great empty space that only the brilliant solution devised by Brunelleschi was capable of covering.

The directors of construction that succeeded Arnolfo di Cambio were Andrea Pisano, Francesco Talenti, and Giovanni di Lapo Ghini; Arnolfo is believed to have been responsible for the sides and the triple-aisle body of the building, which may have been constructed to a somewhat less grandiose design than what we see today. Of the four great bays, the first two correspond to the original basilica of Santa Reparata (see no. 6). Along the sides, a reticule of polychrome marble emphasizes the structural components: the right side is older, and it served as a model to the remaining portions, which were not completed until the fifteenth century.

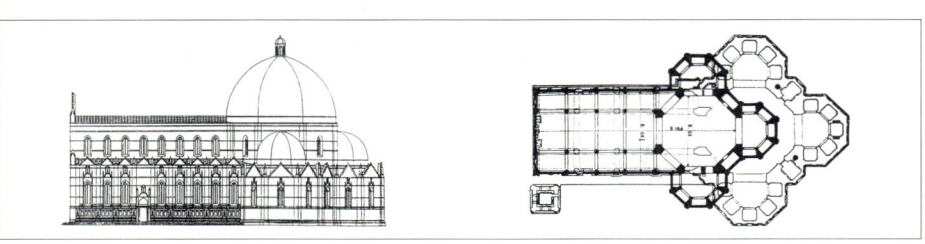

Florence during the Gothic Period

37
Belltower of the Cathedral (or Giotto's Belltower)
1334-57
Giotto and others
Quartiere San Giovanni, Piazza del Duomo

Standing nearly eighty-five meters tall, this great tower was begun forty years after work had begun on the Cathedral, to which it constitutes a vertical complement. It is based on a cross-section some fifteen meters square, reinforced at each of its four corners by octagonal volumes. The style of each of the three artists who succeeded, one after the other, as supervisors of construction, can be clearly distinguished in the three different vertical segments.

The lowest section, which is attributed to Giotto, appears as a closed volume, divided by polychrome bands and panels. The intermediate section is by Andrea Pisano, and it features niches with statues, windows, and loopholes. Lastly, the uppermost part (the work of Francesco Talenti) has two-light and three-light mullioned cuspidate windows, which conclude the ascending sequence; and this is the section in which the architectural motifs are most radically different from those found on the sides of the Cathedral. Throughout the height of the tower — unlike in the building by Arnolfo di Cambio — the surface treatment is tricolored, with an alternation of red, green, and white marble.

38
Loggia of Bigallo
1352-58
Alberto Arnaldi
Quartiere San Giovanni, Piazza del Duomo

In this structure, which is made up of three bays that are open on two sides, orphans — which were known as "bigallini" — were left. Later modifications were made — plenty of them and some of them quite major — until the radical restoration which was carried out in the second half of the nineteenth century, resulting in the reclamation of the fourteenth-century features, such as the jutting roof, the two-light mullioned windows and the arches, which were partly sealed up during modern times.

39

Church and Convent of Santa Maria Novella
1278-1360
Quartiere Santa Maria Novella, Piazza Santa Maria Novella

Beginning in the second half of the thirteenth century, through a similar sequence of events, the Dominican complex took shape in a location that was opposite and symmetrical to that of the church of Santa Croce. The body of the original church of Santa Maria delle Vigne, founded in the tenth century and corresponding to what is now the transept, served as the foundation for the final plan of the great church, based on the Cistercian examples, such as that adopted in Santa Trinita. On the interior, the space is divided into a nave and two aisles, where arches and vaults puntuate the presence of seven bays, with an elongated span: the last of the seven corresponds to the transept, where it intersects with a similar system of vaults and bays. While serving to emphasize the structural components, the grey stone ribbing gives a special thrust to the architectural composition as a whole, with a clear Gothic influence; a special and distinctive note emerges from the traditional interplay of arches and vaults, here supported by an original combination of solidity and lightness, powerful pillars and slender semi-columns. During the course of the fourteenth century, the front was not completed (see no. 85), but the three cloisters that run along the left-hand side of the church were completed. The best known, of course, is the "Chiostro verde," or Green Cloister (named after the prevailing shade found in the frescoes); completed around 1350, the round arcades of the quadriporticum seem to hint at a late use of Romanesque motifs. Linked to this cloister is the Gothic "Cappellone degli Spagnoli," adjacent to the "Sala del Capitolo," decorated with frescoes depicting the stories of Saint Dominick.

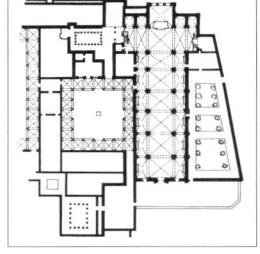

40
Church of Santa Trinita
Ca. 1250-1380
Quartiere Santa Maria Novella, Piazza Santa Trinita

On a far smaller scale than the current version, the complex of the Vallombrosani was founded in the eleventh century. Then, after 1250, a plan for rebuilding and expansion slowly took shape. If we leave aside the façade (see no. 135), the project was completed — probably under the supervision of Neri di Fioravante — during the last quarter of the fourteenth century: and the current, modern-day appearance of the church corresponds to the last phase of this long process of rebuilding, especially on the interior. The Gothic structure is particularly evident in the four bays, punctuated by pillars, the last of which forms part of the transept, in accordance with a plan which is found also in the church of Santa Maria Novella, built at roughly the same time. In the Vallombrosan church, despite a smaller extension of the aisles, upthrusting ogival arches support the sequence of cross vaults, which ends in the square apse, with a two-light mullioned window providing illumination.

41
Church of San Carlo dei Lombardi
1349-1404
Neri di Fioravante and Benci di Cione
Quartiere Santa Croce, Via de' Calzaiuoli

This church, which was originally dedicated to Saint Michael, was rededicated in the seventeenth century to Saint Carlo Borromeo. The structure has preserved its original simplicity, despite all the subsequent renovations: the façade, made of "pietra forte", has a triangular structure, with small crowning arches. The interior, on the other hand, has only a single nave, terminating in a tripartite choir, divided by pillars.

42
Gate of San Niccolò
1324
Oltrarno, Piazza Poggi

This is the only city gate that preserves its original height, and on the interior the passages which once led to the battlements of the city walls are still intact. More than a true gate, however, this structure served as a tower defending the gap through which the river Arno flowed. For this purpose it was connected with the twin tower "della Zecca," located on the opposite bank of the river.

43
Gate Romana
1326
Oltrarno, Viale Petrarca

This is the only city gate that was not isolated from the city walls in modern times; it now stands in the heart of a long stretch of intact walls, running through Oltrarno. Despite the various renovations (the keep has been lopped off, the side passageways were added in the nineteenth century), it has partly preserved its fourteenth-century flavor.

44
Gate of San Frediano
1332
Oltrarno, Viale Ariosto

Also known as Pisana Gate or Carraia Gate, this gate is the largest of its kind. Attributed to Andrea Pisano, who is believed to have completed it in 1332 to 1334, its has a large fornix at its center, nowadays partly sealed up, originally more than thirteen meters in height; the original wooden doors still survive, studded with a dense covering of nails.

45
Church of San Francesco in Fiesole
Beginning in 1330
Fiesole, Salita San Francesco (near the Public Gardens)

In a solitary position on the summit of the hill, and formerly the site of the fortress of Fiesole, stands the church founded by the Romites. From 1405 on, this church was integrated into a Franciscan complex. The restorations done in the early twentieth century highlight, especially on the interior, its Gothic character, at the expense of the fifteenth-century style (which can however still be glimpsed in the cloisters adjacent to the church).

46
Charterhouse of Galluzzo (or of Florence)
Beginning in 1342
Jacopo Passavanti and others
Galluzzo, Via Senese

At the summit of the hill of Montaguto, on the site of an ancient castle, stands this Carthusian complex, the result of a generous subvention on the part of the families of the Acciaioli and the Visconti. Over a considerable span of time, and certainly no earlier than the sixteenth century, the convent was completed with further additions: among these was the sixteenth-century church of San Lorenzo, built by Giovanni Fancelli in accordance with classical modules. The Charterhouse proper was an active teaching center — at least until the suppression under Napoleon — and possessed a library, an art gallery, and a pension for young students; the Gothic *Palazzo degli Studi*, or Hall of Studies, was devoted to this purpose; it consists of three large vaulted halls, set in sequence. The highly articulated structure of the buildings is based around a central space, which was unified by a quadriporticum at the end of the fifteenth century. The Charterhouse, and its inward-looking plan, served as inspiration to Le Corbusier in his design for the convent of La Tourette.

47

Pontevecchio
1345
Neri di Fioravante (?)
Between the Lungarno Acciaioli and Via Guicciardini

This bridge corresponds to the site of the earliest bridge in the city, which existed during Roman times and was rebuilt more than once. The current structure was rebuilt following the Second World War, in conformity with the model that was built following the disastrous flooding of 1333. With the construction of the double row of shops, an image took form that was quite unlike the bridge's appearance in the Middle Ages: it was no longer part of the city fortifications, with the apparence of a castle, it had become a road running over a bridge, intended as a civil structure that was an integral part of the city's everyday life. In 1565 Vasari's Corridor (see no. 119), set atop one of the two rows of shops, completed the physiognomy of the bridge; in the years that followed, the Pontevecchio — together with the Cathedral and Palazzo Vecchio — formed a stereotypical component of the Florentine landscape. In the second half of the sixteenth century, goldsmiths began to take over the shops, which had till then been owned and used by butchers; in the seventeenth century, the shops were enlarged with new back-rooms, which were supported by wooden rafters. Thus two fundamental components of the identity of the Pontevecchio were combined.

48

Palazzo dei Giudici (or Castellani)
First half of the 14th century
Quartiere Santa Croce, Piazza dei Giudici, corner of Lungarno Diaz

This building was originally joined with the Castello di Altafronte, which was later destroyed during one of the floods of the Arno. The fourteenth-century façade is composed of a basement with rusticated arches; above that is a three-storey series of centered windows; from 1574 to 1841 this building housed the Giudici di Ruota, or Magistrates of the Rota (hence, its name); thereafter it become the site of the Museum of the History of Science.

49
Palazzo dell'Arte dei Beccai
First half of the 14th century
Quartiere Santa Croce, Via Orsanmichele 4
The plaster in this case conceals the stone, but not the handsome layout of the façade, with square windows alternating with centered windows and doors; the butchers' guild set up their offices here after 1318, rebuilding a tower-house of the Macci family, later presidium of the Captains of the nearby church of Orsanmichele. From the sixteenth century on, it was the building of the Arte dei Fabbriceri.

50
Palazzo Davanzati
Ca. 1350
Quartiere Santa Maria Novella, Piazza dei Davanzati
Some critics have ventured an attribution to Arnolfo di Cambio. The fact remains, however, that this is a piece of architecture from the "mature fourteenth century," even though it constitutes a thirteenth-century-style expansion of a merchant's home: the plan, in fact, is based around a courtyard with an external staircase leading to the various floors.
The façade was originally organized into three stories, rising above a considerable rusticated basement (the crowning loggia structure was added in the sixteenth century): with its sequence of windows with basket-handle arches, the elevation was later to constitute a "model of tradition" to which architects and builders turned for new building forms, especially for the fifteenth-century palazzo.
The fairly drastic restoration that was done around 1905 and 1906 was intended to emphasize its character as a typical Florentine home of the fourteenth century, with the consequential elimination of the transformations that the palazzo had undergone over time.

51
Orsanmichele (or Church of San Michele in Orto)
1337-1404
Simone Talenti and others
Quartiere Santa Croce, Via de' Calzaiuoli

Built as a loggia in which to hold the grains market, the building was raised following 1367 and transformed into a house of worship in the lower section, while continuing to serve as a grain storehouse in the upper section (in the two very high upper stories, the Notarial Archives were installed in 1569). The mastermind behind this transformation was Talenti, who filled in the arches of the loggia, creating a series of blind three-light mullioned windows, modelled — in the earliest years of the fifteenth century — in accordance with the style of the flamboyant Gothic. Set on the pillars of the structure are the tabernacles with statues of patron saints of the Guilds: the transformation into a house of worship was sponsored and approved by the guilds themselves, whose headquarters were located in the surrounding neighborhood.

On the ground floor is the church, rectangular in shape, divided into two aisles by square pillars. One can enter the two large upper rooms from the Palazzo dell'Arte della Lana (together, the two buildings form the headquarters of the Società Dante Alighieri, as a consequence of the restoration done during the early twentieth century. See no. 202).

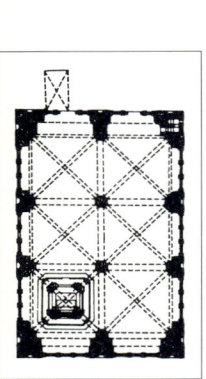

52
Palazzo Acciaioli
Second half of the 14th century
Quartiere Santa Maria Novella, Borgo Santi Apostoli 8

Known also as the "Palazzo della Certosa," since it belonged to the family that largely financed the construction of the complex at Galluzzo. Thoroughly restored at the end of the nineteenth century, when the stone facing was restored, this palazzo features the simple layout of a building style that was heavily influenced by public norms and regulations.

Florence during the Gothic Period

53
Palazzo Canigiani
Second half of the 14th century
Oltrarno, Via de' Bardi 28-30
In the façade made of living stone, a number of distinctive features of fourteenth-century construction can be seen: the regularity of the doors and windows, the linear layout. The courtyard, on the other hand, has a structure and a form of expression that alludes to a number of features typical of the fifteenth century.

54
Palazzo dei Capitani of the Guelf Faction
14th-15th century
Quartiere Santa Maria Novella, Piazza San Biagio
This building features a complex stratification of projects and designs that, beginning with the earliest thirteenth-century nucleus, expanded its size and modified the façades over the course of the fourteenth century. Toward the year 1420 Brunelleschi added a new wing, corresponding to the great assembly hall; Vasari was responsible for the small hanging loggia added in 1589 on the side of Via del Capaccio.

55
Loggia della Signoria (or dei Lanzi)
1374-81
Benci di Cione and Simone Talenti
Quartiere Santa Croce, Piazza della Signoria
The many names that have been given to this structure (including Loggia dell'Orcagna) are indications of the many functions that it has served over the years: meeting place and site of public pronouncements, headquarters of the public guards, and lastly showcase for the Medici collections *en plein air*. Its large round arches allude to styles and proportions of the fifteenth century.

BUILDINGS NOT IN MAP

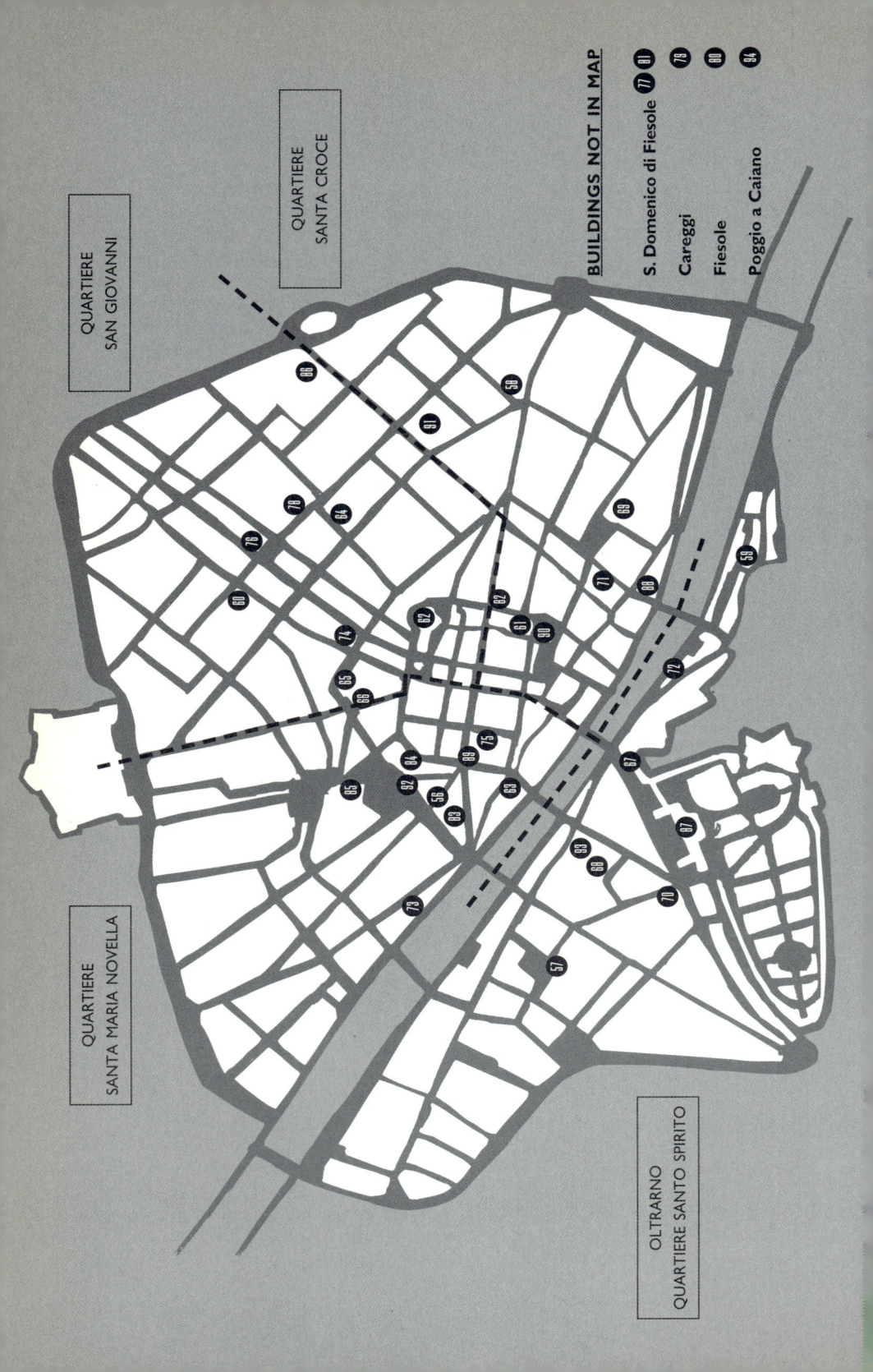

- **S. Domenico di Fiesole** 77 81
- **Careggi** 79
- **Fiesole** 86
- **Poggio a Caiano** 94

QUARTIERE SAN GIOVANNI

QUARTIERE SANTA CROCE

QUARTIERE SANTA MARIA NOVELLA

OLTRARNO
QUARTIERE SANTO SPIRITO

Florence during the time of Brunelleschi

The personality and work of Brunelleschi greatly overshadows the Florentine stage, exerting an influence that continued well after the architect's death in 1444. Brunelleschi brought the city an array of radically new concepts which nonetheless maintained a respectful adherence to the examples set by the ancients; this is a "dichotomy" that was quite typical of early Humanist architecture. And in that school of architecture Florence attained a standing of unrivalled supremacy. We can say that Leon Battista Alberti is the ideal expression in the second half of the Quattrocento of the crying need for a practical and theoretical formulation; in the same sense, we can say that Brunelleschi marks a watershed dating from the dome of the Cathedral: the year was 1418 and, in terms of archetypes, the *novitas* was at dialectic odds with the local architectural tradition, which had risen to an extremely high level of order and logicm and had done so precisely in the construction of the great church of Santa Maria del Fiore. Cosimo de' Medici intended to reclaim the northern section of the city of Florence, through a series of major building projects, such as the churches of the Santissima Annunziata and San Marco: all funded through the great generosity of Cosimo de' Medici, under the supervision of Michelozzo, the trusted architect to the Medici prince. The principal axis ran along the Via Larga, where the family palazzo was under construction: Michelozzo, in this context, completely deserves credit for having defined the building style of the Florentine city palazzo. The palazzi of the Pitti, the Strozzi, and the Rucellai were to constitute so many significant variants on that style. When Lorenzo the Magnificent died, and the Florentine Republic was restored (1494), these events also marked the end of the great chapter in Florentine Humanism.

56
Former Church of San Pancrazio (Rucellai Chapel and Marino Marini Museum)
1375-1470
Quartiere Santa Maria Novella, Via Federighi
This was the church of the Rucellai family; around 1465 they commissioned Alberti to completed its Gothic structure; in the family chapel he reproduced the form of the temple of the Holy Sepulcher. After serving in a complex succession of roles (in the nineteenth century it was used as a tobacco-processing plant), the interior, equipped throughout with intermediate floors, has been the site of the Marino Marini Museum, ever since the Seventies.

57
Church of Santa Maria del Carmine
1268-1475
Oltrarno, Piazza del Carmine
Begun in the thirteenth century, this church of the Carmelites was completatated in 1475 with an appearance that hearkens back to the fourteenth century. The great fire of 1771 triggered the great renovations of the late eighteenth century (see no. 160): the outer shell of the building survived the fire in its then unfinished state, while on the interior only the chapel that Masolino, Masaccio, and Lippi painted for Felice Brancacci survived.

58
Church of Sant'Ambrogio
14th-15th century
Quartiere Santa Croce, Via Pietrapiana
Founded in paleo-Christian times, this church was rebuilt in a number of phases, and was completed in 1486: while the façade (redone in the nineteenth century) is Gothic, the light simplicity of the interior evokes a fifteenth-century style, emphasized by four Renaissance altars. Noteworthy is the termination of the nave, in an arch enclosed by two side chapels.

59

Church of San Niccolò sopr'Arno
First half of the 15th century
Oltrarno, Via San Miniato
Perhaps the only indicator of the Romanesque origins of this church, founded in the eleventh century at the edge of a marshy area, is the bare triangular façade, with a central rose window; the fifteenth century reconstruction can be sensed in the interior with its single nave, covered by trusses, and ending in a noteworthy tripartite presbytery.

60

Monastery and Refectory of Santa Apollonia
Ca. 1380-1450
Quartiere Santa Maria Novella, Via San Gallo 25 and Via XXV Aprile 1
Founded in the eleventh century, the convent of the Camaldolite nuns bears features that testify to the phase of rebuilding and expansion in the fourteenth and fifteenth centuries; among them, showing clear influence of Brunelleschi's work, is the dining hall (known chiefly as the "Cenacolo," or Refectory), which was frescoed by Andrea del Castagno in 1450 in accordance with strict criteria of uniformity with the architecture.

61

Chiostro degli Aranci in the Abbey of Florence
1435-40
Bernardo Rossellino
Quartiere Santa Croce, Via Dante Alighieri
The quadriporticum, with its rectangular shape, is constituted by the stacking of a double Ionic order with basket-handle and puteal arches in the center: despite a number of uncertain points, the architectural language clearly belongs to the height of the Renaissance, and the form of the bays, corresponds to Brunelleschi's "cube," in all likelihood, intentionally.

62
Dome of the Cathedral (Santa Maria del Fiore)
1418-34
Filippo Brunelleschi (with Lorenzo Ghiberti)
Quartiere San Giovanni, Piazza del Duomo
This building was also a symbol of a profound conceptual and artistic turning point, a watershed constituted by the personality and work of Brunelleschi, who provided the plan as a preliminary construction sketch, developed conceptually with the use of mathematical calculations. The reader may well be aware of the events leading to Brunellschi's receiving the commission, following the competition established by the "Arte della Lana," or Woolworkers Guild in 1418, after all the efforts to span the enormous empty space (the interior diameter was 42 meters) by more traditional methods of construction (see no. 36). If one considers also the thoroughly unusual height of the project (82 meters from the top of the intrados to the cathedral floor), which made it impossible to build the ribbing and scaffolding, then one clearly sees the need facing the builders to develop a structure that would be "self-supporting" during each and every step of construction. The Florentine architect conceived of this structure as an octagonal two-fold dome supported by a tambour; working together with Ghiberti, Brunelleschi designed the two walls in stone in the lower part, and in "herring-bone" masonry in the upper part, following a model copied from the ancients. A series of large ribbings join the two walls and, sheathed in white marble on the exterior, announce the cupola's impressive volume; divided into eight huge sectors, Brunelleschi's huge "engine" was not only fully in accordance with the scale of the city skyline, but became that skyline's unrivalled star. The cupola was completed in 1434; high atop it is the finishing touch, the lantern completed by the Florentine architect, inspired by Vitruvius's concept of the weather tower.

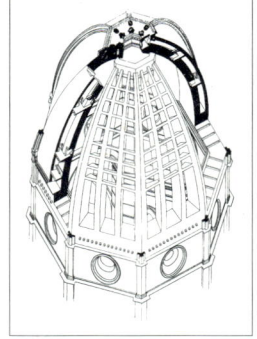

Florence during the time of Brunelleschi

63
Sacristy of Santa Trinita
1419-23
Filippo Brunelleschi (with Lorenzo Ghiberti)
Quartiere Santa Maria Novella, Via di Parione
In what was once the chapel of Onofrio Strozzi, the style of Ghiberti can be recognized in the portal and, on the exterior, in the elongated windows: with the powerful ribbings set above the light-colored masonry walls, the architecture of the interior is reminiscent of Brunelleschi's concept of unified space.

64
Ospedale degli Innocenti, or the Foundling Hospital
1419-26
Filippo Brunelleschi and others
Quartiere San Giovanni, Piazza della Santissima Annunziata

Funded by the "Arte della Seta," or the Silkworkers' Guild, the construction of this Foundling Hospital was one of the first great works completed by Brunelleschi. Despite the addition of an additional storey in 1438, the portico facing out over the piazza constitutes a remarkable statement of a principle. This portico also constitutes a model that has been widely adopted over the course of the fifteenth century: set at the top of the staircases, the portico's nine round arcades transmit to the exterior the modular cadences of so many "spatial cubes," on the interior of the portico, covered with groin vaults. They appear on the façade, above the slender Corinthian columns which — together with the ribbing of the arches and the string-courses that connect with them — emphasize the decidly geometric layout of the composition as a whole. The same architectural motif can be seen in the first cloister and in the five bays that make up its two sides.

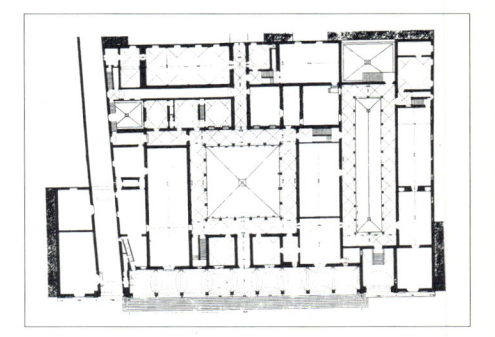

65
Church of San Lorenzo
1419-60
Filippo Brunelleschi and others
Quartiere San Giovanni, Piazza San Lorenzo
Built in the fourth century, and rebuilt during the Romanesque period, the church building as we see it today bears the form that Brunelleschi impressed upon it. Aside from the issue of architectural stratification, the church has become famous due to the remarkable succession of artistic events, which began in the fifteenth century and ended in the seventeenth century; the church is a product of the generosity of the Medici, who chose San Lorenzo as their family temple and pantheon. Here, as in so many other great Florentine churches, the stark, unfinished façade seems to serve as an artistic counterweight to the lushness of the interior, where all of the Medici's most important architects were summoned to make their contributions. (see no. 109 and no. 144) Brunelleschi was commissioned in 1419 to reorganize the existing structure, still detectable, in the plan with a nave and tzo aisles and a transept. He was successful in his attempt to set the existing features within a geometric grid, previously established in accordance with the canons of a new architecture. In the context of the new order, the most outstanding features were the large stone Corinthian columns that support the round arches, thus punctuating the space according to a regular rhythm, establishing the rhythm of the bays in the two side aisles. The same rhythm appears in the chapels with large arched pediments that open along the perimeter. As is the case in so many other buildings by Brunelleschi, the central cupola underlines the effort being made to centralize the space, which seems to clash with the Latin-cross plan, imposed by the many existing structures.

Florence during the time of Brunelleschi

66
Barbadori Chapel in the Church of Santa Felicita
1425
Filippo Brunelleschi
Oltrarno, Piazza Santa Felicita
Brunelleschi set, alongside one of the oldest churches in the city, a square aedicule, covered with a cupola: the form and the size give it more in common with a sacristy than with a chapel. Its location, alongside the façade, caused an overall change of the plan, which was then implemented in the sixteenth and eighteenth centuries (see no. 167).

67
Sagrestia Vecchia of San Lorenzo
1420-29
Filippo Brunelleschi
Quartiere San Giovanni, Piazza San Lorenzo

At one of the two ends of the transept of San Lorenzo, Brunelleschi built a cubic space covered by a hemispheric cupola: this is an elementary composition capable of expressing, within the context of a central plan, a number of the canons of architecture "in the manner of the ancients." Many observers have seen in this structure one of the most important affirmations of the art of the early Renaissance.

A more thorough study, however, reveals some very complex pieces of architecture amidst the simplicity of the overall plan: some instances are the large lunettes, the spandrels, and the other figures used to join the two volumes. The layout is then emphasized by the stone ribbings, overlaid upon the white of the plaster. Around 1440, Donatello worked on the decoration of the church, which, one may note, is particularly well integrated into the architectural structure. Donatello is responsible for the tondos and medallions in the upper section of the church, above the central trabeation.

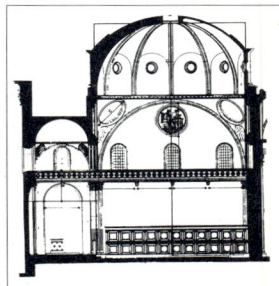

68
Church of Santo Spirito
1446-88
Filippo Brunelleschi and others
Oltrarno, Piazza Santo Spirito

This church is traditionally considered to be the most exquisitely distinctive of Brunelleschi's religious buildings: in any case, it is the only one that was built *ex novo*, unrestricted in planning and construction by any existing elements. Designed in 1434, construction did not begin until twelve years later; the Manetti, Giovanni da Gaiole, and Salvi d'Andrea all took part in the building of this church, making considerable alterations in the original plan, especially on the outer structure which had at first been conceived as a succession of apsidioles. Yet, despite the modifications that the design underwent, the plan appears in all the sharp clarity of its original conception, and constitutes a sort of manifesto in stone of the architectural principles of Humanism. In this connection, one should note the interior, based on a module of eleven Florentine "braccia" (translator's note: the "braccio" was an Italian unit of measurement ranging from fifteen to thirty-nine inches); this module is used along the perimeter creating four separate bays. Here, just as in the church of San Lorenzo, the tall monolithic Corinthian columns punctuate the vast space, creating a three-aisle structure that occupies both the central part and the transept. Unlike the building of San Lorenzo, however, the space in this church appears equivalent along each of the sides: despite the shape of a Latin cross, the church takes on the structure of a central plan, in which one of the arms simply seems to have become longer. As in so many of the great Florentine buildings of the fourteenth and fifteenth centuries, the façade appears unfinished: broken up by the central oculus and by the tortuous crowning structure, its unadorned surface seems almost to hint at the intricate geometry to be found within.

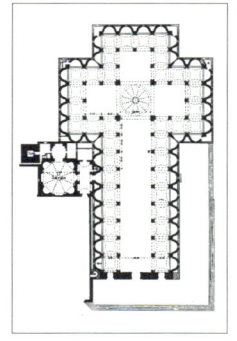

Florence during the time of Brunelleschi

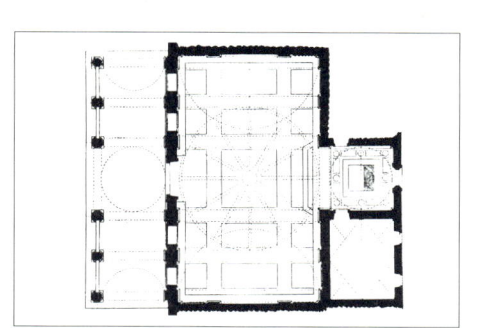

69
Chapel of the Pazzi and the Great Cloister of Santa Croce
1430-73
Filippo Brunelleschi and others
Quartiere Santa Croce, Piazza Santa Croce
The renovation of the convent began sometime after 1423, in the wake of a very serious fire; based upon a double order of arcades, the larger cloister was completed in 1453. In the section of the church that escaped damage in the fire, between the terminal chapels and the fourteenth-century cloister, stands the chapel that Brunelleschi designed in 1442 for Andrea Pazzi: this chapel was conceived as a rectangular space which was inscribed within a circle, corresponding to the hemispheric cupola. The chapel's volume is configured as a central plan, perfectly calibrated to a series of geometric modules, and the structure was completed by one or more of the assistants of the Florentine master architect (Michelozzo, Manetti, or Giuliano da Maiano). A different architect, however, was responsible for the elegant portico: it envelops the entire façade, incorporating the motif of the central arcade as an element of interruption in an square-paneled attic on columns. The name of Rossellino has been mentioned in this connection, perhaps inspired directly by Alberti himself.

70
Church of San Felice in Piazza
Ca. 1457
Michelozzo
Oltrarno, Piazza San Felice
The medieval church was radically renovated, beginning in the middle of the fifteenth century; the façade dates from that era, and is crowned by a tympanum, as does the interior, covered by trusses and punctuated by large windows. The part with a cross-vault ceiling dates from the sixteenth century.

71

Palazzo Bardi
1410 (?)
Filippo Brunelleschi (?)
Quartiere Santa Croce, Via de' Benci 5
Of particular interest is the courtyard where, according to tradition, a young Brunelleschi was to appear uncertain and in any case in the grip of the "logic of transition" (from the Gothic to the Renaissance): the arcades appear to be soaring but, at the same time, compressed in accordance with a sequence that has yet to show the rhythm of the porticoes of the fifteenth century.

72

Palazzo Capponi da Uzzano
1427
Lorenzo di Bicci
Oltrarno, Via de' Bardi 23
The façade overlooking the road appears to be divided into two parts that constitute two separate phases: the lower section has an emphatic and distinctively fourteenth-century style rustication, while the upper section is smooth and features ashlars cut in *opus quadratum*. A noteworthy feature is also the courtyard set upon octagonal columns, in the center of the building.

73

Palazzo Lenzi-Quaratesi
Ca. 1430
Michelozzo (?)
Quartiere Santa Maria Novella, Piazza Ognissanti 2
More than the documents, the similarities with a number of the villas of the Medici caused scholars to suggest the name of Michelozzo as the architect of this prototype of Florentine civil architecture (and this is true chiefly of the sequence of centered windows); here, as in the nearby Palazzo Ricasoli, the architecture with projecting elements still seems linked chiefly to fourteenth-century motifs.

74
Palace of Cosimo de' Medici
1444-69
Michelozzo
Quartiere San Giovanni, Via Cavour 1
According to tradition, Cosimo the Elder preferred this plan to the one built by Brunelleschi across the way from the church of San Lorenzo. Michelozzo proposed a great cube, set at the mouth of Via Larga, its core "carved out" by a space that corresponds to the central courtyard; with its façades made of stone ashlars, ordered upon three floors separated by string-course cornices, and with a regular sequence of two-light mullioned windows and the crowning cornice, the trusted architect of Cosimo thus set forth a model of civil construction that was to be extensively copied and quoted, as it were. Prior to the subsequent renovations (see no. 158), Vasari describes the palazzo in its original appearance, punctuated by the bays and two-light mullioned windows, distinguished by a hanging garden that, on the west side, extended to the first floor. Between 1449 and 1469, Michelozzo built the "Cappella dei Magi," or Chapel of the Magi, named for the renowned fresco by Benozzo Gozzoli: this space with a rectangular plan still preserves the original purity of its plan.

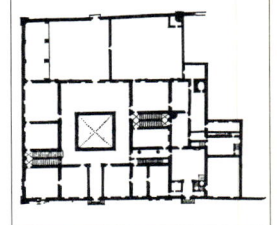

75
Palazzo dello Strozzino
1451-69
Michelozzo
Quartiere Santa Maria Novella, Piazza Strozzi 2
This attribution is based chiefly upon similarities with Palazzo Medici, from which it takes the tripartite layout of the façade and the motif of the progressive thickening of the ashlars, far more marked in the lower section; set upon two arcades per side, the façades of the courtyard reproduce this three-fold sequence. The building was completed by Giuliano da Sangallo.

76
Church and Convent of San Marco
1437-52
Michelozzo

Quartiere San Giovanni, Piazza San Marco
This is a crucial project in the larger urbanistic strategy of Cosimo the Elder, who was determined to reclaim the northern section of the city. Here, Michelozzo was entrusted with the restoration and transformation of a complex dating from the thirteenth and fourteenth centuries, which had originally belonged to the Silvestrini, since ceded to the Domenicans of the Osservanza. Cosimo's architect preserved, of the original church, the main hall, to which he added {tribuna} and the polygonal apse, as well as raising the presbytery. The new church was dedicated in 1442; the interior as it appears now is largely the product of baroque renovations. The hand of Michelozzo appears much more clearly in the convent: in 1451 the courtyard adjacent to the church was completed, the cloister of Sant'Antonino, which incorporated the refectory and the hospice, joining them with the new sleeping quarters. And it was here, on the light-colored spans of wall on the upper floor, that Fra' Angelico painted his very well known series of frescoes. Lastly, we should examine the cloister of San Domenico, entirely designed by Michelozzo, behind the body of the church. Between the two cloisters, rendered uniform by an elegant portico with basket-handle arches, stretches the Library: this is a space split up into three naves by a double file of Ionic columns, designed to accommodate collections of art open to the public (it is traditionally said to be the first structure designed for this purpose). This convent was associated in history with the name of Savonarola, who launched his campaign of moral reform from here.

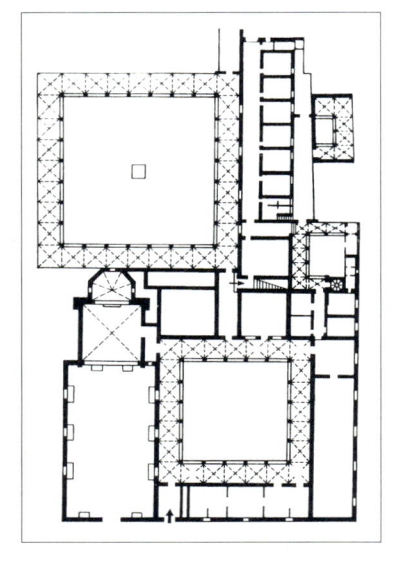

77
Church and Convent of San Domenico in Fiesole
Ca. 1419-38, 1480-90
Michelozzo and Giuliano da Maiano
San Domenico di Fiesole

Michelozzo began work on the renovation of the cloisters during and following the construction of the complex of San Marco, which was built for the Dominicans. The attribution of the design of the church is based, on the other hand, on a number of similarities to other buildings by Giuliano; one should note in particular the interior with a single nave and three chapels on each side, with frontal arches made of decorative stone.

78
Church and Convent of the Santissima Annunziata
1444-76
Michelozzo and others
Quartiere San Giovanni, Piazza della Santissima Annunziata

Michelozzo was given the job of "modernizing" the fourteenth-century complex by the Servites: working first in the atrium (or "Chiostrino dei voti," literally, "Little Cloister of Vows"), and later in the larger cloister, he borrowed the motif of the colonnade of Palazzo Medici with large cross vaults set upon basket-handle arches. In the extended space of the Sacristy, we find once again the large vaults set upon flying buttresses, like those found previously in the convent of San Marco.

Better known, and quite controversial, is the work done on the Gothic nave, where a polygonal choir built on a central plan was rudely inserted, taking inspiration from Brunelleschi's design of Santa Maria degli Angeli.

The violent debate that arose drove Ludovico Gonzaga, who was financing the work, to replace the architect after 1455: between that date and 1476, first Manetti, and later Alberti worked on the building, transforming Michelozzo's polygonal choir into a rotunda surrounded by nine chapels.

The portico that faces the piazza was completed at a later date (see no. 140).

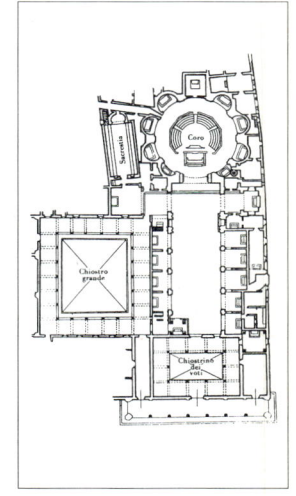

79
Villa Medici a Careggi
1457-82
Michelozzo
Careggi, Viale Pieraccini 17

This building came about through the renovation of a structure purchased by Cosimo the Elder, but its reputation was established by Lorenzo the Magnificent, who selected it as the headquarters of the Accademia Platonica. Evidence of this intellectual splendor can be found in particular in the arrangement of the gardens. This structure lies midway between Florence and the Mugello, where the category of the fortified structure had found noteworthy expression in the residences of the Cafaggiolo and the Trebbio: Careggi represents the transition toward the "villa di delizie," or "holiday villa," which was later codified in the projects by Sangallo. We find features typical of the lower Middle Ages, such as the crenellated balcony that crowns the façades. In particular, the logical arrangement of all the rooms in a U-shaped plan constitutes the most noteworthy new aspect. Of later date was the little side loggia that many attribute to Giuliano da Sangallo: heavy renovations were carried out during the sixteenth century, partly because of the serious damage that the building suffered after the expulsion of the Medici.

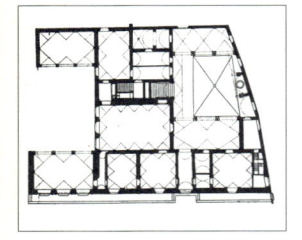

80
Villa Medici in Fiesole (or Il Palagio)
1457-61
Michelozzo
Strada Vecchia Fiesolana

All traces of the medieval style have been banished here: the rigid grid not only indicates the arrangement of the interior spaces but also the façades of the villa which had been conceived — prior to the expansion in the eighteenth century — as a perfect cube. Orchards and gardens surround the building, divided into large terraces, reflecting the same geometric order.

81
Abbey of Fiesole
1456-64
Assistants of Michelozzo
San Domenico di Fiesole, Via di Badia
This medieval church (see no. 10), set on the steep slope of the hill, was transformed through the generosity of Cosimo the Elder; of particular interest is the relationship between the plan and the arrangement on different levels, underlying which is a complex system of cellars, dormitories, and hanging gardens. Set on relatively high ground, the structure of the church stands at an angle to that of the convent, which is in turn organized along two separate axes of symmetry.

The program of ecclesiastic reformation, inspired by the constructions of Brunelleschi, is quite clear: to rebuild the medieval structure in the form of a classical *templum* with a single nave and a barrel-vault roof. The original concept, however, was modified in view of a series of structural problems, and thus two lateral wings and series of chapels, not planned on at first, were subsequently added.

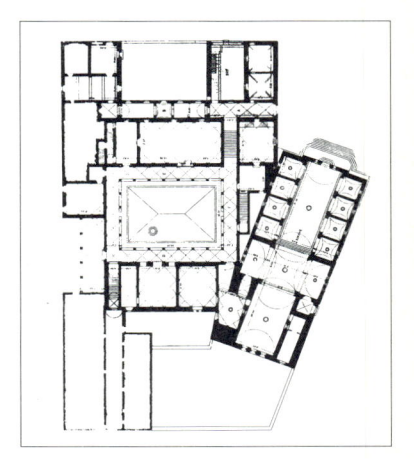

82
Palazzo Pazzi
1458-69
Giuliano da Maiano
Quartiere Santa Croce, Via del Proconsolo 10
Here one finds a number of refined variations on the traditional layout of the fifteenth-century palazzo: in this façade arranged over three stories, above the irregularly rusticated base, the two-light mullioned windows with mouldings and with original carved decorative motifs, stand out. The same type of windows are found in the courtyard, occupied on three sides by a colonnaded portico.

83
Palazzo and Loggia Rucellai
1446-51 and 1460-66
Leon Battista Alberti and Bernardo Rossellino
Quartiere Santa Maria Novella, Via della Vigna Nuova 18

Leon Battista Alberti was asked by the exceedingly wealthy banker Giovanni Rucellai to transform this family residence and to provide it with a new façade. He designed it (and Rossellino built it) in stark contrast with Michelozzo's model of a Florentine palazzo. There was thus no middle ground with the medieval tradition; rather an uncompromizing affirmation of the canon of Vitruvius: the uniform flat ashlars of the basic surface are framed by the three stacked orders of pilaster strips — Ionic, Doric, and Corinthians, so as to compose a perfect recreation of a palazzo "in the manner of the ancients." Each of these panels contains large two-light mullioned windows, set inside arches with radial ashlars, conveying an unmistakable flavor to the whole. The same innovative energy emerges ten years later in the three arcades of the loggia; set facing the palazzo, it is intended as a site to be used for family ceremonies.

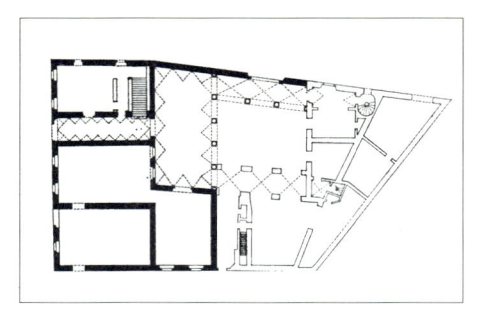

84
Palazzo Antinori
1461-66
Giuliano da Maiano
Quartiere Santa Maria Novella, Piazza degli Antinori 3

In its chilly elegance, the square façade is broken up into regular ashlars of "pietra forte"; the placement of the main door establishes a relationship with the base of the square based on the golden section. This is a further demonstration that the underlying architectural conception of the building, aside from whatever archaic features the façade may possess, was profoundly rooted in Humanistic principles.

85
Facade of the Church of Santa Maria Novella
1439-42
Leon Battista Alberti
Quartiere Santa Maria Novella, Piazza Santa Maria Novella

This project sprang from an entirely secondary objective: the intention had been to cover the fourteenth-century building with a new façade (see no. 39). And yet this is one of the most important pieces of architecture to have risen during the Florentine Quattrocento; entirely bound up with the architect who was also author of the treatise *De re aedificatoria*, it was to establish an archetype for religious buildings for many centuries to follow. In its lucid two-dimensional conception, the façade truly embodies a remarkable instance of adaptation of the Renaissance *novitas* to the Florentine tradition: the Gothic structure is encased in a geometric layout, based on an exceedingly rigorous grid of modules, with an execution in accordance with the customary two-tone alternation of marbles. In all likelihood, it was the Rucellai family, who were financing the project, that arranged for the commission to be given to Alberti, the scion of a family that had been expelled from Florence for political reasons.

86
Palazzo Scala-della Gherardesca
Ca. 1472-90
Giuliano da Sangallo
Quartiere San Giovanni, Borgo Pinti 99

What chiefly survives of the palazzo built for Bartolomeo Scala, a humanist and the Cancelliere, or chancellor, of the Florentine Republic, are the façade overlooking the gardens and the courtyard decorated with terracotta bas-reliefs. Despite the renovations done during the eighteenth century, we can still recognize numerous references to the villa of Poggio a Caiano, which Giuliano worked on during the same years.

87
Palazzo belonging to Luca Pitti
1457-70
Luca Fancelli
Oltrarno, Piazza Pitti

The fifteeth-century section, which was commissioned by the enormously wealthy banker Luca Pitti, consists of the seven central bays, punctuated on all three stories by round-arch windows set against an entirely rusticated background. The design, which is traditionally attributed to Brunelleschi (1440), was actually built after his death, with clear intentions of rivalry, if not perhaps of antithesis, with the building then under construction for the Medici family; there is certainly a topographical antithesis (Palazzo Pitti lies just to the south of the hill of Boboli) as well as a stylistic antithesis (less traditional in manner than the building by Michelozzo, and in any case, the work of an architect who had seen one of his plans rejected out of hand by Cosimo the Elder). And yet, when it was later purchased by the Medici and transformed into a grand-ducal palace (see no. 120), the building conserved both the original name of the fifteenth-century structure, and the original architectural modules, set out with philological precision, in the new, expanded façade.

88

Palazzo Horne
Ca. 1480-90
Giuliano da Sangallo or Cronaca
Quartiere Santa Croce, Via de' Benci 6

In the absence of solid documentation, attributions have been made based on similarities of style: similarities with Palazzo Gondi above all, particularly in the austere layout of the façade. The courtyard with a portico along only one side, and with a loggia on the first floor, is clearly a piece of original design. This building now houses a museum holding the collection of the late proprietor, an English art critic named Herbert Horne.

89
Palazzo Strozzi
1489-1534
Giuliano da Sangallo, Cronaca and others
Quartiere Santa Maria Novella, Piazza Strozzi

Beginning with Vasari, architectural critics and historians have traditionally attributed this building to Benedetto da Maiano, who supposedly conceived of it "in competition" with the palazzo built by the Medici in the same period of time (the wealth of the banker Filippo Strozzi was said to be greater than the quite considerable estate of Lorenzo). Here too we find the rustication punctuated by two-light mullioned windows, and topped with a quite emphatic cornice: in the plan and in the volumetric connection of the great complex structure, which was rigorously organized around a central courtyard, it would seem that the most important figure was that of Antonio da Sangallo the Elder, who completed a wooden model. Critical to the actual construction, however, during the period from 1490 to 1498, were the master craftsmen under the supervision of the Cronaca: and this factor may well explain the presence here of frequent references to the fourteenth-century tradition, according to recent critical thought. The enlargement toward Piazza Strozzi, dating from 1533-34, is attributed to Baccio d'Agnolo.

Today the building is public and houses cultural institutions and exhibition space.

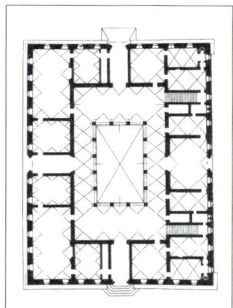

90
Palazzo Gondi
1490-1501
Giuliano da Sangallo
Quartiere Santa Croce, Piazza San Firenze, 1

In this building, designed for Leonardo Gondi, we see a reiteration of the distinctive features of Florentine civil architecture of the fifteenth century, as codified by Michelozzo: the outer face made of rusticated stone, the jutting cornice, the plan arranged around a courtyard. Substantial modifications were made in the nineteenth century by Giuseppe Poggi.

91
Church of Santa Maria Maddalena de' Pazzi (or of Cestello)
1481-1500
Giuliano da Sangallo
Quartiere Santa Croce, Borgo Pinti
In this Cistercian complex, the best known feature is the quadriporticum that serves as the vestibule of the church. This quadriporticum is one of the most highly acclaimed pieces of architecture ever produced by Humanism. Here, for the first time we know of, Giuliano employed the motif of the partly trabeated portico, a clear piece of inspiration from the models of Leon Battista Alberti and, in any case, unquestionably influenced by the antiquarian style; particularly striking is the harmonious punctuation of the composition as a whole. It was completed in 1492, and includes the original columns with Ionic capitals "with a dropping pulvino." The regular, unvarying sequence is unbroken, save for the two large arches set on a straight line with the portal that served as the main entrance to the church.

This church was built in the fifteenth century, and was partly remodelled over the following two centuries. The interior is built with a single nave, with series of chapels running along either side. After the damage caused by the flood in 1966, the building was generally repaired and restored to the way it had been in the early Renaissance.

92
Loggia of San Paolo
1489-96
Quartiere Santa Maria Novella, Piazza Santa Maria Novella
Located directly across from the great façade designed by Alberti, the loggia concludes the great piazza created in the thirteenth century, in the tradition of stage design. With its nine round arches, its tondi, and its stone members, it is based on Brunelleschi's model of the Foundling Hospital.

Florence during the time of Brunelleschi

93

Sacristy of Santo Spirito
1488-97
Giuliano da Sangallo and Salvi d'Andrea
Oltrarno, Piazza Santo Spirito

This is a temple with a grid plan, possibly inspired by the Baptistery; the cupola, shaped like an eight-faced umbrella, was rebuilt by Salvi d'Andrea after it collapsed once. The Sacristy is connected to the church by a vestibule with barrel vaults running parallel to the central nave.

94

Villa Medici at Poggio a Caiano
1485-94, 1515-19
Giuliano da Sangallo
Poggio a Caiano, Via Pistoiese

Built at the orders of Lorenzo, who personally took part in designing it, this villa is considered by many to be an archetype in its category. The architecture has been shorn of defensive elements, and there is a prevailing reference to the treatise by Alberti: the plan is based on a square, in fact, and employs simple but rigorous relationships of proportion. The composition is further broken up into three sections, two of which are set around the central building, which in turn acts as the nucleus of the distribution of the space. And it is here that the symmetrical axis is found, serving also as an entry axis, underscored by a loggia with Ionic columns and a pediment with a polychromatic frieze: this entire assembly is set in the main façade, and is one of the most original features of the work. Diverging sharply from traditional models, the loggia here forms part of the upper structure, which is supported by a porticoed basement; the loggia thus become a continuous terrace surrounding the "piano nobile," or main floor.

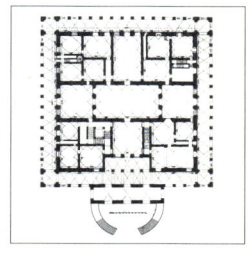

75

QUARTIERE SAN GIOVANNI

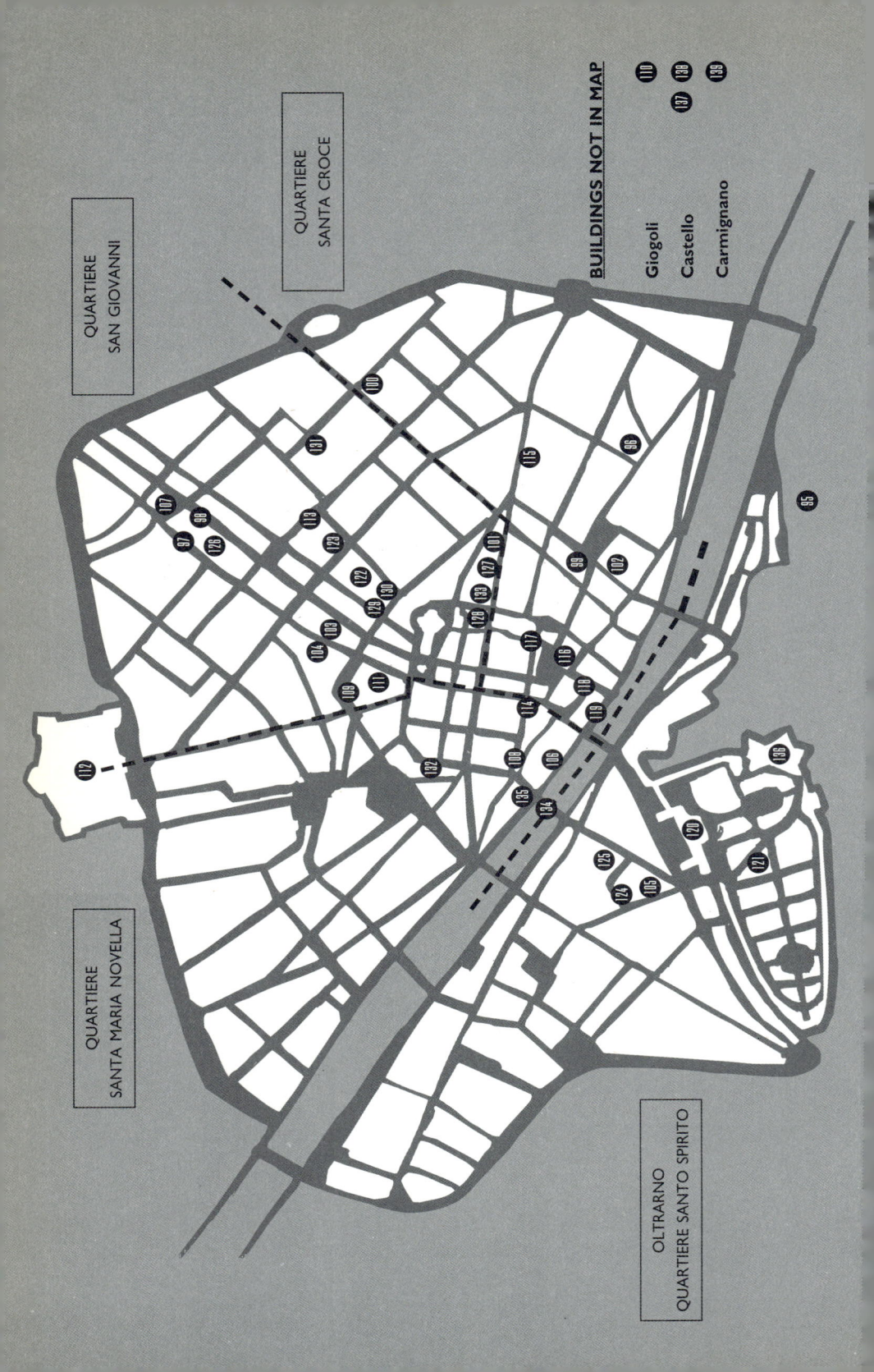

QUARTIERE SANTA CROCE

QUARTIERE SANTA MARIA NOVELLA

OLTRARNO
QUARTIERE SANTO SPIRITO

BUILDINGS NOT IN MAP

Giogoli — 110
Castello — 137, 138
Carmignano — 139

Florence during the Cinquecento

Lorenzo de' Medici, known as Lorenzo the Magnificent, died in 1492, and with him perished the project of a radical *renovatio Florentiae*. No longer the epicenter of humanistic culture in Europe, Florence at this point seems to have been wavering between two extremes of expression; on the one hand, there was a turning inward, to a tradition of autochthonous style, particularly clear in civil construction, and, on the other hand, the return to classical models of architecture. Through the creations of such artists and architects — working independently — as Raphael, the Sangallos, and Michelangelo, Florence established new ties to papal Rome, the new capital of the Reniassance. This crisis of identity was in part a reflection of the tortuous political affairs and the exasperating oscillation — between 1494 and 1530 — of republican government and Medici seignories. After proclaiming himself the grand duke of Tuscany, Cosimo I consolidated various forms of absolute power over the city, as is shown by his decision in 1540 to establish his own residence in the historic seat of the city's self-government, the Palazzo dei Priori. Cosimo imposed a sort of "language of the state," through the figure of the personal architect of the prince; on the basis of this mandate, Vasari organized a large-scale system that joined, through a long corridor, Palazzo della Signoria with the palace that once belonged to the family Pitti. A similar fiduciary relationship was later to link — just as Cosimo and Vasari went together — first, Francesco I and Bernardo Buontalenti, and then Ferdinando I and Bartolomeo Ammannati; even though in these other cases, the working bond was to yield far less ambitious fruit.

95

Church of San Salvatore al Monte (or San Francesco al Monte)
Ca. 1500
Cronaca
Oltrarno, Viale Galilei

An addition to the fifteenth-century Franciscan convent, this is a church of exceeding simplicity, in accordance with the general trend of the Republic: one can glimpse a certain antiquarian taste both in the façade, which culminates in a tympanum, and on the interior, which has a single nave, along which runs a double order of pilaster strips.

96

Church of San Giuseppe
Ca. 1520
Quartiere Santa Croce, Via San Giuseppe

Very simple in its plan, this church is organized around a single nave and flanked by side chapels that expand its central space; this is an approach that we are to find later in other buildings of the early sixteenth century. The façade, which betrays a clear baroque influence, dates from the middle of the eighteenth century.

97

Church of San Giovannino dei Cavalieri
Ca. 1550
Quartiere San Giovanni, Via San Gallo

Originally a fourteenth-century oratory dedicated to Saint Mary Magdalene, the building was radically transformed by the knights of the Order of Malta. The unusual façade, on the surface of which stand the emblems of the Knights of Malta, encloses a vestibule that in turn gives access to the interior of the church; in the three-aisle plan, punctuated by round arches, one can still glimpse the fourteenth-century structure.

Florence during the Cinquecento

98
Cloister of the Scalzo
Beginning of the 16th century
Quartiere San Giovanni, Via Cavour 69
The elegant, self-contained porticoed courtyard is all that remains of the convent of the Confraternita degli Scalzi: the architectural structure is punctuated by slender columns that, whether single or twinned, are a clear borrowing from the model employed by Brunelleschi in the church of Santo Spirito. In the background extend the sacred scenes painted by Andrea del Sarto, one of the reasons for this place's renown.

99
Palazzo Cocchi-Serristori
Ca. 1500
Baccio d'Agnolo or Cronaca
Quartiere Santa Croce, Piazza Santa Croce 1
What seems particularly noteworthy in this façade is the way in which the same layout also includes features dating from the fourteenth century, particularly the stout rusticated pillars on the ground floor; this purpose is served by the Roman arches, made out of brickwork, with clear references to wholly sixteenth-century models.

100
Palazzo Albizi
Ca. 1500
Baccio d'Agnolo or Cronaca
Quartiere Santa Croce, Borgo degli Albizi 12
This large building is overlaid upon medieval building that once stood here: in the façade, which is divided into three stories, appear equally Renaissance features and others closely linked to local tradition. Aside from the jutting roof, one should note the radial ashlarsused on the lower floor, and the windows framed by flat ashlarwork in the upper floor.

101
Palazzo Panciatichi-Ximenes
Ca. 1500
Giuliano and Antonio da Sangallo the Elder
Quartiere San Giovanni, Via Giusti 17-27
This palazzo was originally designed by the architects as their own residence; despite the enormous size, the two façades show a harmonious conception of the relationship between solid and empty space, and between surfaces and elements of ornamentation. Extensively remodelled during the course of the seventeenth century, the palazzo was the residence of Napoleon during the general's stays in Florence.

102
Palazzo Corsini-Serristori
Ca. 1500
Baccio d'Agnolo
Quartiere Santa Croce, Borgo Santa Croce 6
More than the façade overlooking the road, which boasts no significant aspects, the courtyard nicely sums up the transition between the fifteenth and the sixteenth centuries: note the unusual sequence of portico and through-portico, where we find Corinthian capitals, shaped by the inventive flair of Baccio d'Agnolo with special volutes.

103
Palazzo Taddei
1503-04
Baccio d'Agnolo
Quartiere San Giovanni, Via de' Ginori 19
With its simplicity of layout, this façade was to become a model for the builders of the sixteenth century. Particularly noteworthy is the courtyard, where one can glimpse artistic juxtapositions: alongside the fifteenth-century loggia are columns with "palm-frond capitals" a typical signature of Baccio's work. The niches and statues, on the other hand, are seventeenth-century additions.

Florence during the Cinquecento

104
Palazzo Ginori
Ca. 1510
Baccio d'Agnolo
Quartiere San Giovanni, Via de' Ginori 11
In this building, probably of medieval origin, the work of Baccio d'Agnolo is visible in the many classical features, set in an exceedingly simple layout (one should note, for example, the loggia created in the façade). The interiors still feature large seventeenth- and eighteenth-century decorations.

105
Palazzo Guadagni
1503-06
Cronaca
Oltrarno, Piazza Santo Spirito 10
In its stark simplicity, this building appears to be in keeping with the atmosphere of the Republic and its recurring exhortations to severity of manner. The loggia on the upper floor seems to give a new spaciousness to the close-set sequence of windows that occupy the lower floors; the graffiti, as well, set in the lower panels served to lighten the composition.

106
Palazzo Rosselli-del Turco
Ca. 1517
Baccio d'Agnolo
Quartiere Santa Maria Novella, Borgo Santi Apostoli 17-19
In its bare simplicity, marked only by stringcourses and by the stone-block centering, the long façade is extremely representative of the Republican period; with an explicit rejection of humanistic architectural language, Baccio was attempting here to hearken back to the city's tradition, presenting it in a more modern form.

107
Palazzo Pandolfini
1515-20
Raffaello and the circle of Sangallo
Quartiere San Giovanni, Via San Gallo 74

This structure marks the return of interest in antiquarian models that coincided with the papacy of Leo X, of the family of the Medici: many have seen this palazzo, built for the bishop Giannozzo Pandolfini, as a bit of "Roman architecture" inserted into a Florence that was uncertain about its artistic direction.
In the building, designed by Raphael and probably built by Giovanni Francesco and Aristotele da Sangallo, a great many inventions of architectural language succeed one another along the lengthy and asymmetrical façades: we find windows with curvilinear or triangular fronts, in the midst of a refined repertory of classical references, which — among the panels, stringcourse, and balustrades — set it apart from other examples of civil architecture.
In the corners and around the portal, the large rusticated ashlars, with their irregular shapes, stand out, providing an intentional contrast with the regular geometric uniformity of the façades.

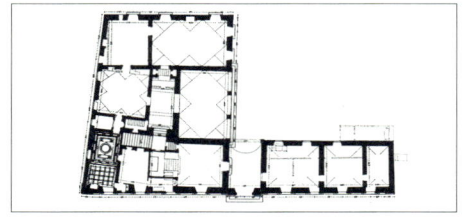

108
Palazzo Bartolini-Salimbeni
1517-20
Baccio d'Agnolo
Quartiere Santa Maria Novella, Piazza Santa Trinita 1

This was considered to be Baccio's masterpiece; here he developed a series of linguistic innovations: in an elevation rendered uniform by the "pietra forte" appear the distinctive crossed windows, with their own order of pilaster strips, trabeation, and tympanum. The entire façade fits into the atmosphere of the "return to the classical," that was so typical of the years of transition to the Medici principality.

109
Sagrestia Nuova of San Lorenzo
1519-34
Michelangelo Buonarroti
Quartiere San Giovanni, Piazza San Lorenzo

Pope Leo X made the decision to complete the structure that had been left unfinished by Giuliano da Sangallo, who intended it as a mausoleum for the remains of Lorenzo the Magnificent. Michelangelo was given the commission of remodelling it as a sepulchral chapel for the Medici family; it is located at the right-hand extremity of the transept, and hence in a symmetrical position with respect to the sacristy built by Brunelleschi, allowing observers to make a direct comparison between the two great masters. The initial approach is similar: both began with a cube sealed by a hemispheric cupola; Michelangelo, however, gave the structure greater vertical thrust: this is made possible by the courses set under the large lunettes, as well as by a wide array of mechanisms of perspective, such as the modelling of the windows according to the vanishing points and the caissons of varying size set in the intrados of the cupola.

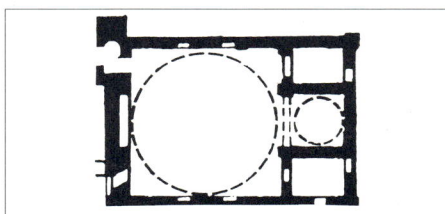

110
Villa I Collazzi
1534
Giogoli, Strada Volterrana

It is hard to say just who designed this further Romanist project, often attributed to Michelangelo. One thing certain is that, with its plan in the shape of a C and with its stacked loggia, the villa built for the Dini family features the same model used by Peruzzi in the Farnesina. Long left unfinished, the building was completed and expanded around 1935.

111
Biblioteca Laurenziana, or Laurentian Library
1519-59
Michelangelo Buonarroti
Quartiere San Giovanni, Piazza San Lorenzo
Michelangelo's original plan broke this structure into two spaces, the vestibule and the reading room, conceived as independent spaces in succession. In the first room, an accentuated sense of verticality prevails, and can be seen reflected in the curtain walls, which are treated as full-fledged façades (here, the outlined windows alternate with pairs of inset columns). The vestibule is completed at the center by the monumental staircase built by Ammannati in accordance with an original architectural model: it leads into the rectangular reading room where Michelangelo reinterpreted the well-consolidated model of the *libraria*. The series of chairs is punctuated, along the side walls, by lesenes and windows in cornices.

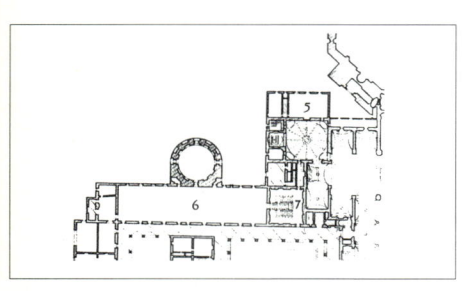

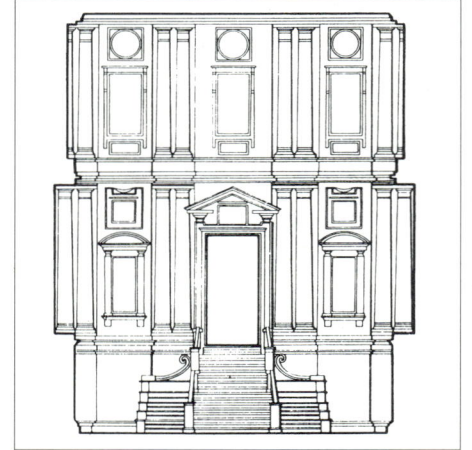

112
Fortezza da Basso (or Fortress of St. John the Baptist)
1534-35
Antonio da Sangallo il Giovane
Quartiere Santa Maria Novella, Viale Strozzi
This fortress was built to a pentagonal plan, at the order of Alessandro de' Medici, who wished to use it as a bulwark against internecine foes. The outer wall of this "dictatorial fortress" is partly covered with a special rustication featuring globes and diamond tips, and includes a number of previously existing structures, such as the thirteenth-century Faenza Gate.

113
Portico of the Confraternita dei Serviti
1516-25
Antonio da Sangallo il Vecchio
Quartiere San Giovanni, Piazza della Santissima Annunziata
Built by craftsmen under the supervision of Sangallo, this building formed part of a larger project of homogenization of the architecture surrounding the piazza, which is dominated by the presence of the portico of the Foundling Hospital, or "Ospedale degli Innocenti." Therefore, Brunelleschi's work was knowingly taken as a model, with the borrowing of architectural rhythm and cadence.

114
Loggia del Mercato Nuovo, or Loggia of New Market
1546-64
Giovanni Battista del Tasso
Quartiere Santa Maria Novella, Via Gate Rossa
In one of the sites in the city traditionally set aside for the marketplace stands this structure built at the orders of Cosimo I; intended for trade in gold and silk, the loggia has a square plan with three-four arches per side. Solid stone columns support the large ribbed vaults, dividing the space up into equal parts, each of which corresponded to a different category of trade.

115
Loggia del Pesce, or Loggia of the Fish
1567
Giorgio Vasari
Quartiere Santa Croce, Via Pietrapiana, corner of Via Buonarroti
This building was moved here and reassembled, following the demolition of the Mercato Vecchio at the end of the nineteenth century. In accordance with a recurring module in other Florentine late-Renaissance loggias, the architectural structure is based on a double row of arcades, which are in turn supported on columns of the Tuscan order.

116

Ducal Palace (enlargement of the Palazzo Vecchio)
1495-1590
Cronaca, Giorgio Vasari, Bernardo Buontalenti and others
Quartiere Santa Croce, Piazza della Signoria

After the fifteenth-century transformations of the building planned and built by Arnolfo di Cambio, a new drive for expansion came from the new Republic, and the need for a great hall in which to hold assemblies. Thus, on the eastern side of the building, the Salone dei Cinquecento, designed by Cronaca, was built: Leonardo da Vinci and Michelangelo were commissioned to decorate it, complying with an objective that was emphasized later as well in the great artistic competition ("to make of the palazzo a spectacular container for the art of Florence"). The watershed came about with the establishment of the principality (1532): first, under the supervision of Baccio, later under Giovanni Battista del Tasso, and from 1555 onward under the direction of Vasari, the *"quartieri monumentali"* — or monumental quarters — took shape; these were splendidly decorated and frescoed residences, each created for different members of the family of the grand duke. These apartments were arranged on three stories along the perimeter of the block stretching from the Via della Ninna (where the first wing stands), to the Via de' Leoni and the Via de' Gondi. More than anyone else, Vasari left a profound and theatrical imprint here, that is limited intentionally to the interiors alone; the exterior will remain tied to the same sober ideals of the fourteenth-century building. The same approach was taken later by Buontalenti, who was commissioned after 1588 to give a definitive and unified appearance to the architectural exterior. Palazzo Pitti soon replaced this building as the residence of the grand duke; this palazzo, now called Palazzo Vecchio, or the "old palazzo," remained a heritage from the past, before being used as the chambers of the Italian parliament, and finally as the Florence City Hall.

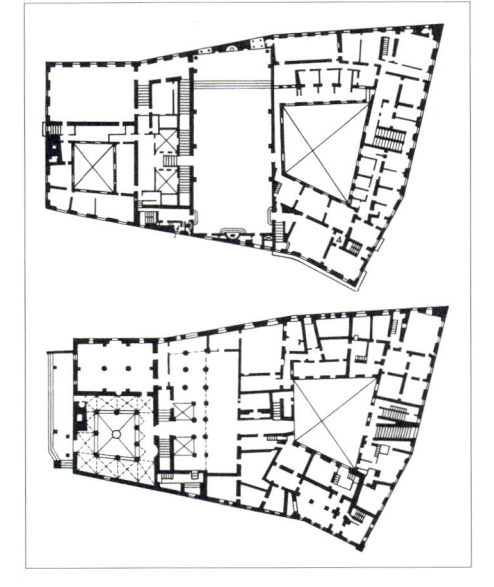

Florence during the Cinquecento

117
Palazzo Uguccioni
Ca. 1550
Circle of Sangallo
Quartiere Santa Croce, Piazza della Signoria 7

The twin semi-columns, the courses of trabeation, and the tympanums over the windows constitute a façade designed in conformity with an impeccable classical language. It is no happenstance that this is the first significant case of *renovatio* of the grand-ducal piazza in accordance with a plan that was to be completed with the fountain of Neptune and, above all, with the wing of the Uffizi.

118
Uffizi
1559-80
Giorgio Vasari and others
Quartiere Santa Croce, Piazza della Signoria

The decision to build an urban telescopic structure, so to speak, stretching from the river Arno to the renovated Piazza della Signoria dates from 1546. Only after Florence's victory over Siena (1555) and consolidation of its territorial holdings did the city proceed with the construction of the building intended to house the offices needed for the expanding bureacracy, and especially for the "Uffizj dei Tredici Magistrati." Vasari's idea had an urbanistic application, and it hinged on an urban space that functioned both as a road and as a courtyard. A *promenade architecturale* that relied for its effect upon the contrast between plaster and stone, and was flanked by two nearly symmetrical curtain walls appearing to culminate toward the river in a loggia, highlighted by a large Venetian window.

After the death of Vasari (1574), supervision of the work was taken over by Buontalenti, and later by Alfonso Parigi. Cosimo I first had the idea of assembling many works of art there, making it the nucleus of the public museum that would one day be established by the house of Lorraine.

119

Vasari's Corridor
1565
Giorgio Vasari
(running from the Uffizi to the Pitti Palace, across the Pontevecchio)
In order to link the Palazzo della Signoria with Palazzo Pitti, i.e., the chambers of government with the new grand-ducal palace, Vasari built in only five months this airy passageway, which could be adapted to many different urban settings; it served as a portico along the Arno, as a crowning course along the Pontevecchio, and as a loggia overlooking Santa Felicita.

120

Ducal Palace (enlargement of Palazzo Pitti)
1558-77
Bartolomeo Ammannati and others
Oltrarno, Piazza Pitti

The far terminus of the system of grand-ducal residences is constituted by what was once the palazzo of Luca Pitti (see no. 87), purchased in 1549 at the behest of Eleonora de Toledo, the consort of Cosimo I. But it was not until 1556 that Ammannati was commissioned to enlarge and renovate it, so as to create a new grand-ducal residence. Work was concentrated on the courtyard built uphill of the fifteenth-century block of buildings; open on one side facing the hill, the courtyard is the transition point toward the garden in formation, for which it was to constitute the compositional fulcrum. As it was conceived by the architect of Cosimo, the courtyard is primarily the heart of a "Roman style" palazzo, conceived in accordance with the model established by Michelangelo for Palazzo Farnese; its inner façades are punctuated by three orders of rusticated semi-columns (a conceit that is reminiscent of Sanmicheli's work on the gates of Verona).

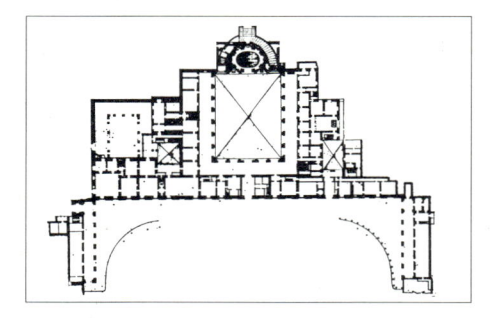

121
Boboli Gardens
1550-88
Tribolo, Bernardo Buontalenti and others
Oltrarno, Piazza Pitti

The project of a grand-ducal palace would have been incomplete without a great park; behind the palazzo a large "Italian-style" garden took shape, with terracing and flowerbeds to take advantage of the natural slope of the hill of Boboli. The arrangement of the garden was begun by Tribolo and, after he died in 1550, continued with Ammannati, who conceived it as a compositional integration of the palazzo. From the sixteenth-century courtyard, the true center of the organizational plan, extends an axis of symmetry along which one finds the *Amphitheater*, used for shows (the steps date from the seventeenth century), the *Fishpond of Neptune* and other antiquarian inventions.

In a panoramic setting, in remarkable surroundings of plantlife and nature, amidst statues, fountains, and architectural *divertissements*, the sixteenth-century section of the park thus developed (corresponding to the northern section alone, in the area between the palace, the fortress, and the "garden of the knight.") Buontalenti, who took over in 1583, designed and built the *Grottoes*, a fanciful architectural capriccio mingling motifs of nature (stalactites, stone foliage...) and specific references to the classical tradition. The garden was extended in the 17th century to its current size of 45,000 square meters: the project was overseen by Alfonso Parigi and other architects working on the expansion of the palace, demonstrating once again the organic links between the two areas of the vast estate.

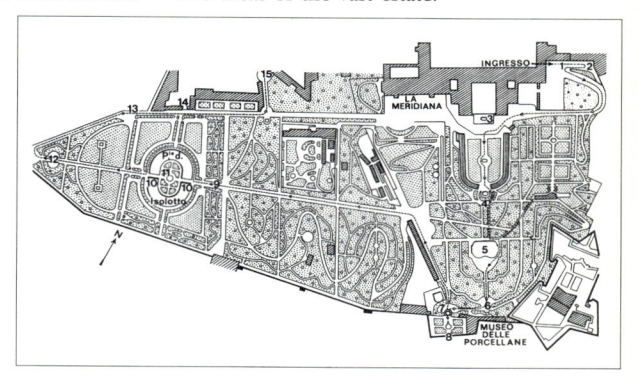

122
Palazzo Niccolini
Ca. 1550
Circle of Baccio d'Agnolo and Giovanni Dosio
Quartiere San Giovanni, Via de' Servi 15
This palazzo can be attributed more to Baccio's school (Domenico) than to Baccio himself. The façade is, in any case, believed by some to represent a sixteenth-century that is openly "without architectural order"; the plan however features an unusual approach, with two courtyards, in the second of which the large porticoed front was a later project completed by Dosio.

123
Palazzo Grifoni (or Budini-Gattai)
1557-63
Baccio d'Agnolo and Bartolomeo Ammannati
Quartiere San Giovanni, Piazza Santissima Annunziata, corner of Via de' Servi
Another "Roman-style" palazzo; in the brick façades, this aspect appears emphasized by the repertory of windows with tympanums and large string-course cornices, as well as by the reduction of the rustication to a corner element. Baccio designed the floor plan while Ammannati designed the elevations, and then oversaw the construction of the building.

124
Palazzo Capponi in Oltrarno
1559-85
Bernardo Buontalenti and others
Oltrarno, Via Santo Spirito 4
Of particular interest here are the façade overlooking the "lungarno" and the rear façade, which has been attributed to Buontalenti. Remarkable bits of invention can be seen especially in the architectural accessories: brackets and cornices of windows, string-courses, little pilasters and capitals with volutes, in which many have indicated features typical of the mannerist style.

125
House of Bianca Cappello
1567-70
Bernardo Buontalenti
Oltrarno, Via Maggio 26
This house belonged to the mistress of Francesco I, the Venetian woman Bianca Cappello; a reconstruction of an existing fifteenth-century structure, this building is one of the few surviving examples of a "graffiti" decorative motif, which was so common in the late sixteenth century. Buontalenti, who was an alchemist and an occultist, lavished the decorations with a wide array of monsters, winged fauns, and devils.

126
Medici Casino
1568-74
Bernardo Buontalenti
Quartiere San Giovanni, Via Cavour 57
At a certain distance from the family palazzo and from the center of courtly life, but situated along the traditional Via Larga, this residence of Francesco I was designed as a laboratory in which to engage in the alchemistic experimentation which the grand duke practised along with his architect; in its essential lines, the decorative apparatus seems to be based on models taken from the local tradition.

127
Palazzo Ramirez di Montalvo
1568-72
Bartolomeo Ammannati
Quartiere San Giovanni, Borgo Albizi 26
This building was commissioned by Cosimo's high chamberlain, and it was created by incorporating a number of existing buildings. This is demonstrated by the entrance portal's distance from the center of the façade. At the center of the façade, instead, is a framed window and a large Medici coat of arms, features set in the elevation which can be seen from the Via Giraldi.

128

Palazzo Salviati
Ca. 1565-70
Bartolomeo Ammannati
Quartiere San Giovanni, Via del Corso 6
This building stands on the foundations of houses that once belonged to the family of Beatrice Portinari. The plan was originally arranged around two courtyards; the first of the two, featuring arcades with columns of the Tuscan order, was transformed into a large hall, the second, known as the "Cortile degli Imperatori," or Courtyard of the Emperors, in the form of a peristyle, with two sides featuring porticoes, adorned with statues and busts.

129

Palazzo Pucci
Ca. 1565-70
Bartolomeo Ammannati
Quartiere San Giovanni, Via de' Pucci 6
Built at the same time as Palazzo Salviati (with which it shares a number of details), this building was created by the consolidation of three existing buildings. At the center of the long and massive façade one notes a loggia on the first storey, an unusual element in the range of Florentine architecture.

130

Palazzo Giugni
Ca. 1577
Bartolomeo Ammannati
Quartiere San Giovanni, Via degli Alfani 48
This building, intended for the banker Simone da Firenzuola, displays a simple but well laid out façade that shows clearly a renewed use of motifs typical of "Florentinism." In the light-colored plaster expanses, Ammannati deploys a sequence of portals and ashlars centerings of great plastic quality: one might for instance consider the vertical *suite* set at the center of the elevation.

131
Palazzo Zuccari
1578-79
Federico Zuccari
Quartiere San Giovanni, Via Giusti 43
In the narrow façade in vernacular style, we see rusticated ashlars alternating with smooth strips, with a clear attempt to create dissonance: this refers us to the architect's clear taste for stage-settings; a major figure in late sixteenth-century painting, Zuccari had been summoned to Florence to fresco the interior of the cupola of the Cathedral.

132
Palazzo Larderel
Ca. 1580
Giovanni Dosio
Quartiere Santa Maria Novella, Via de' Tornabuoni 19
The elegant and slightly austere layout of the façade in "pietra forte" hearkens back, and not merely in ideal terms, to Roman-style models of construction: in the façade, broken into three parts by the string-courses, the windows with tympanums and the handsome classical portal stand out, creating a distinctive whole.

133
Palazzo Nonfinito
1593-1604
Bernardo Buontalenti and others
Quartiere Santa Croce, Via del Proconsolo 12
Buontalenti created the emphatically rusticated façade of the ground floor, styling it to the Roman taste; then Cigoli took over, and created the unusual "Palladian" courtyard, with Venetian windows and binate colums. The completion of the façade, punctuated by lesenes in a giant order, was the work of Caccini, possibly with the assistance of Scamozzi.

134
Ponte di Santa Trinita
1567-70
Bartolomeo Ammannati
Between the Lungarno Corsini and the Lungarno Guicciardini
Rebuilt with exacting philological precision after 1945, the bridge was probably based on a model by Michelangelo. Remarkable in its slender gracefulness, the bridge's three long spans have arched profiles and, to emphasize the contrast with the base, they are supported on massive pylons shaped in the form of a double buttress at an acute angle.

135
Façade of the Church of Santa Trinita
1593
Bernardo Buontalenti
Quartiere Santa Maria Novella, Piazza Santa Trinita
The layout of the façade, divided into three parts by a system of pilasters, expresses cadences that are clearly Baroque; in order to give it greater vertical thrust, Buontalenti eliminated from the façade the shapes of the side chapels (see no. 40). His inventions, which can be seen especially in the capitals and in the pediments, confer warmth to an otherwise chilly composition.

136
Forte Belvedere (or the Fort of San Giorgio)
1590-95
Bernardo Buontalenti and others
Oltrarno, Via Costa San Giorgio
Located at the eastern boundary of the Boboli Gardens, this fortress had a complex floor-plan, in accordance with the orography of the site; the star shape complied with what were then the most modern military models of construction. The captain's residence, established as a feature of Medici villas, contained the treasury of the Medici; now it serves as a setting for art exhibitions, along with the surrounding spaces.

137
Villa of Castello
1540-92
Tribolo and Bernardo Buontalenti
Village of Castello, Via di Castello 44-48
This was a Medici estate from 1480 on; the complex was remodelled by the Tribolo, who also designed the garden, supposedly establishing here the archetype of the "Italian-style garden." The subsequent work done by Buontalenti resulted in the portal with rusticated pilaster strips, surmounted by a balcony, the only decorative element for the length of the façade.

138
Villa of Petraia
1576-89
Bernardo Buontalenti
Castello, Via della Pietraia 40
This was originally a little castle owned by the Brunelleschi family; it has kept the original central tower; Ferdinando I ordered it transformed into a Medici villa. Already, Tribolo had laid out an "Italian-style" garden, with terracings and fountains; this garden is the main reason for the villa's reputation.

139
Villa La Ferdinanda
1594-96
Bernardo Buontalenti
Carmignano, village of Artimino
This Medici villa stands atop a wooded hill; a hunting lodge built at the orders of Ferdinando, it came to be something midway between a resort estate and a military fortification. Two corner towers anchor the elongated façade with, at the center, the remarkable hanging loggia that makes the building so distinctive and recognizable.

QUARTIERE SAN GIOVANNI

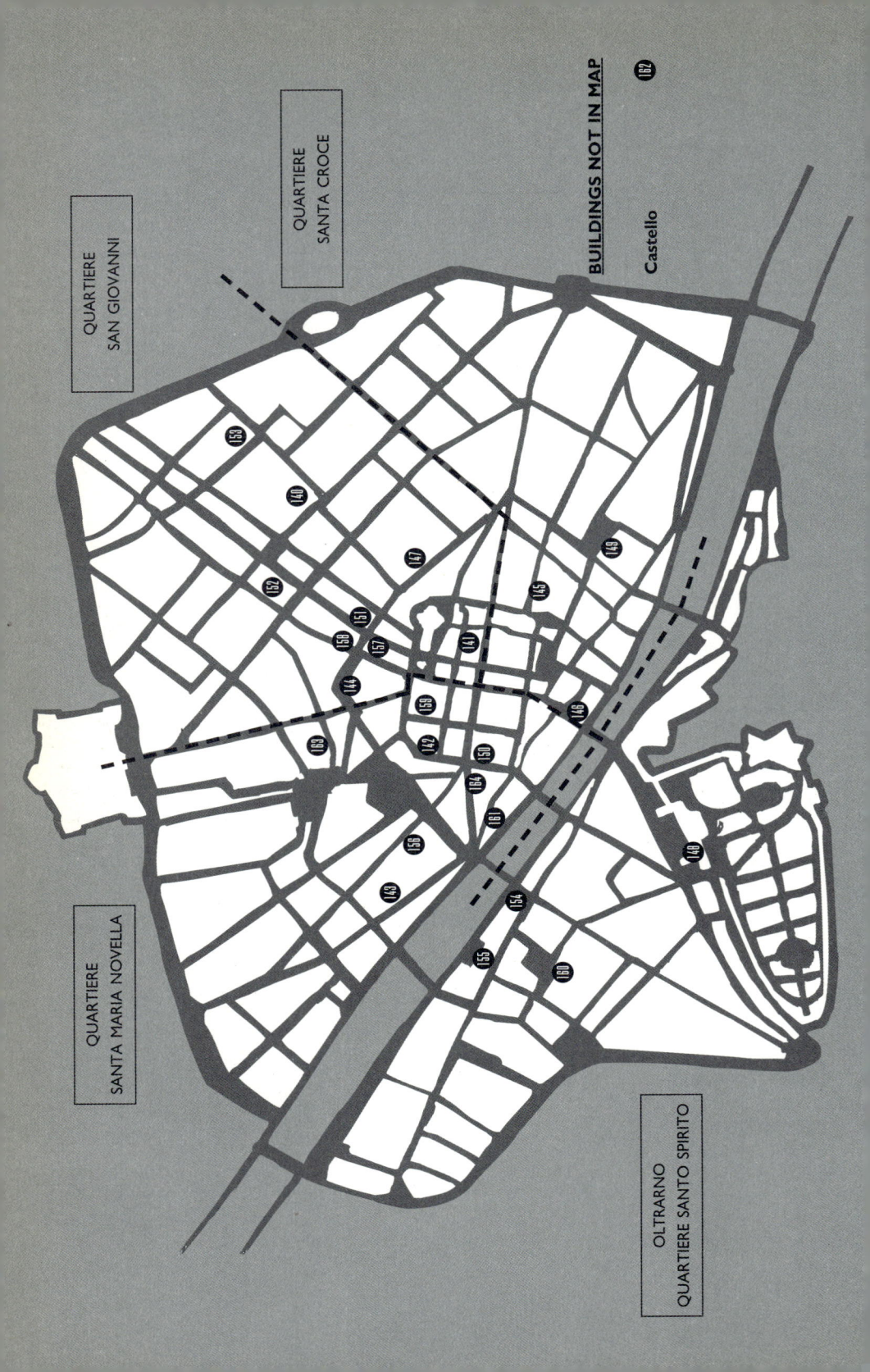

QUARTIERE SANTA CROCE

BUILDINGS NOT IN MAP

Castello 162

QUARTIERE SANTA MARIA NOVELLA

OLTRARNO
QUARTIERE SANTO SPIRITO

Florence during the Seicento

Overshadowed by the legend of fourteenth- and fifteenth-century Florence, by the figures of Giotto, Donatello, and Brunelleschi, baroque architecture was relegated to a fairly marginal area in the city. With the virtuosity of its intarsias, the Chapel of the Princeps, one of the greatest works of the period, was considered a typical expression of the poetics of excess. The critically deplored architecture of seventeenth-century Florence was further denigrated by the ensuing political and economic decline of the city as a whole.

After 1604, with the death of the last grand duke directly descended from Cosimo the Great, Florence seemed definitively relegated to the role of a second-rate capital, haunted by the mediocre personalities of the last of the Medici. Despite all this, the Florentine baroque engendered artists of considerable importance, such as Matteo Nigetti and Gherardo Silvani in the first half of the seventeenth century, Antonio Maria Ferri and Giovan Battista Foggini in the second half.

Church and palazzo remained the themes upon which these architects were generally called upon to work, almost always summoned to renovate, to enlarge, expand, or provide additions, or in some cases merely to do a "restyling" of existing buildings: the repertory of the baroque architect, therefore, almost always consisted of façades, cupolas, lanterns, and — on the interior of the church — edicules, altars, and chapels.

140
Renovation of the Church of the Santissima Annunziata
1601-93
Giovanni Caccini and others
Quartiere San Giovanni, Piazza Santissima Annunziata

Upon the fifteenth-century building (see no. 78) a sort of second church was superimposed, occupying all the most significant spaces with baroque forms (façade and choir, especially). The process began with the façade; redesigning it in the form of a loggia, in 1601-1604, Caccini borrowed and repeated the motif of the single arch, which had previously been erected by Antonio da Sangallo the Young, on an axis with the entrance to the church (see no. 113). In accordance with a theatrical vision of public space, therefore, a third side with loggia was formed, even though the module established by Brunelleschi in the Ospedale degli Innocenti was deformed here in a vertical direction. From 1605 onward, Caccini proceeded to reorganize the choir, providing it with distinctive niches and edicules as a sort of main chapel; in 1608 he remodeled the chapel of Saint Sebastian, linking it directly with the new loggia. The new baroque church was completed under the supervision of Matteo Nigetti in the Coloredo Chapel (1643-52), and finally by Giovan Battista Foggini in the Feroni Chapel (1691-93).

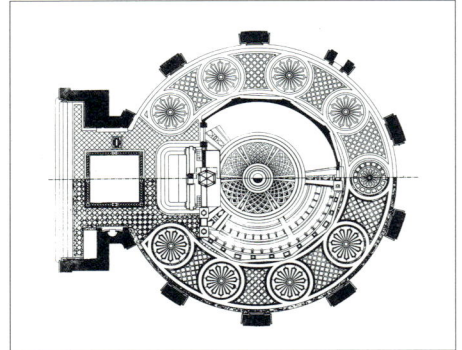

141
Church of the Madonna de' Ricci
1604
Gherardo Silvani
Quartiere San Giovanni, Via del Corso

The forepart of the building which constitutes the main façade was added to the sixteenth-century structure; above the loggia made up of three arches is located the large window that provides illumination to the interior. The balcony, which projects over carved corbels, links them in accordance with a vertical sequence that is reminiscent of the façade of a palazzo. The interior was rebuilt in the eighteenth century by Zanobi del Rosso.

142
Church of the Santi Michele and Gaetano
1604-49
Matteo Nigetti, Gherardo Silvani
Historical center, Piazza Antinori

With its long history of construction, spanning the entire first half of the century, the church of the Teatini is one of the most important pieces of architecture of seventeenth-century Florence; it is no accident that some of the most important artistic figures of the period were involved. The baroque transformation of the medieval façade was completed by Nigetti around 1630; subsequently Silvani enlarged the nave and redesigned the façade in 1648: Counter-Reformation strictness merged here with baroque exuberance, particularly evident in the link between the layout of the façade (with a superimposed double order) and the lavish sculptural decoration (with stone escutcheons, urns, statues in niches...). On the interior, which has a barrel-vault ceiling and is lined with chapels, bas-reliefs alternate with statues; the brightness of the stone contrasts with the background in which the dark tones of the marble predominate. And this is a reflection of the taste in colors that, through the work of Nigetti, we will find in the Medici chapel — built during the same period — in the church of San Lorenzo.

143
Church of Ognissanti
1627-37
Bartolomeo Pettirossi and Matteo Nigetti
Quartiere Santa Maria Novella, Piazza Ognissanti

All that survives of the medieval structure and of the monastery is the bell tower; the original buildings gave the quarter of Ognissanti its name; while the adjacent cloister has preserved its fifteenth-century personality, the church is a perfect example of baroque architecture. With its vertical design, accentuated at the center by the curved pediment, the façade by Nigetti is one of the most original instances of this style.

144

Chapel of the Princeps at San Lorenzo
1604-50
Matteo Nigetti and others
Quartiere San Giovanni, Piazza Madonna degli Aldobrandini

This is the final, and fundamental phase of the Medici plan for the transformation of the church of San Lorenzo into a family pantheon (see no. 65); the construction of this space with a central plan, designed to hold the remains of the grand dukes, was begun in 1604 by Nigetti, perhaps to a plan drawn up by Giovanni de' Medici, and modified by Buontalenti. Here again, there is no communication between the two parts; the new architectural body was added to the building designed by Brunelleschi in accordance with a planimetric and volumetric composition not unlike the one used by Michelozzo in the Santissima Annunziata. The structure is octagonal in shape, and is nearly twenty-nine meters in diameter; the considerable size of the inner space is emphasized by the coloring of the surfaces, covered with dark marble, with intarsias of semiprecious stones, mother-of-pearl, and coral... From the exterior, the volume appears to be covered by a great cupola, fifty-nine meters tall, completed in the middle of the eighteenth century; without a lantern, it is split up into gores like the cupola of the Cathedral.

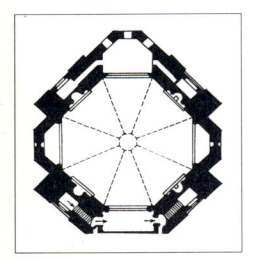

145

Church of Santi Simone e Giuda
1628-30
Gherardo Silvani
Quartiere Santa Croce, Via della Vigna Vecchia

The baroque renovation of this thirteenth- or fourteenth-century church calls upon patterns of great sobriety in this case: the walls of the single nave are punctuated by a network of lesenes and horizontal strips of stone. The simplicity of the interior is counterbalanced by lavishness of the ceiling, covered with gold and punctuated by caissons.

146
Interior of the Church of Santo Stefano al Ponte
1631-55
Pietro Tacca and Antonio Maria Bartolamei
Quartiere Santa Croce, Piazza Santo Stefano

While the crypt was built by the Tacca between 1640 and 1650, the upper section was the work of the client himself, A.M. Bartolamei, working as an amateur architect. In the choir and in the apse, after the weird staircase designed by Buontalenti, appears a broken-line arch silhouette. This curious motif reappears in the niches of the choir and in the bays of the crypt.

147
Hospital of Santa Maria Nuova
1606-63
Bernardo Buontalenti and Giulio Parigi
Quartiere San Giovanni, Piazza di Santa Maria Nuova

This complex was rebuilt in a number of phases, beginning from the original structure and from a series of fourteenth- and fifteenth-century cloisters. Buontalenti was responsible for the design of the portico which unifies the various parts and which includes the fifteenth-century church of Sant'Egidio: the construction of the lower section began with the Parigi, while the upper floor was completed during the early eighteenth century.

148
Enlargement of the Pitti Palace
1619-50
Giulio Parigi
Oltrarno, Piazza Pitti

Following a competition among architects, the grand-ducal palace (see no. 87 and no. 120) was further expanded in the seventeenth century; beginning on the north side (1620), and later on the south side (1631), three new arcades were added to the urban façade, so that, with the addition of two lateral foreparts (1640-50), the "pincer" configuration was attained, as it appears today.

149
Palazzo dell'Antella
1619
Giulio Parigi
Quartiere Santa Croce, Piazza Santa Croce 21
The long façade "a sporti" was entirely painted with a "graffiti" decorative motif; this creation of the Parigi was applied to a building that may have been built by the Buontalenti, and which was created in the sixteenth century by the incorporation of a number of separate buildings. One should note the way in which the intervals between windows are shortened on each of the three stories, progressively toward the termination.

150
Palazzo Strozzi del Poeta
1626-29
Gherardo Silvani
Quartiere Santa Maria Novella, Via de' Tornabuoni 5
This palazzo was commissioned by Giovan Battista Strozzi, a man of letters and patron of the arts, known as "il poeta" — "the poet"; here Strozzi assembled a circle of artists, known as "gli Alterati." The simple layout of the façade is enriched by a number of elegant inventions by the Silvani, such as the little false balconies, the statues on each side, the cornice with metopes and triglyphs.

151
Palazzo Covoni
1623
Gherardo Silvani and others
Quartiere San Giovanni, Via Cavour 4 (6)
In the building as it now stands, which was completed in the eighteenth century, are contained a part dating from the sixteenth century and another that is attributed to Silvani. Here we find fully developed all of the elements in his repertory as a "skilled practitioner of architecture" (Cresti 1990, p. 131): smooth geometric division of the façade in which he sets windows framed and with a tympanum, and an entrance portal with a corbel supporting the balcony above it.

152
Palazzo Castelli-Marucelli
1634
Gherardo Silvani
Quartiere San Giovanni, Via San Gallo 10
A good example of seventeenth-century *mediocritas*, in which the architectural expression is relegated only to the decorative elements of the windows with parapets which stand out against the bare plaster surface: at the center of the façade, one may note the portal with odd carved corbels which hold up the balcony on the first floor. The huge jutting cornice was added in the nineteenth century.

153
Palazzo of San Clemente
Ca. 1640
Gherardo Silvani (?)
Quartiere San Giovanni, Via Micheli, at the corner of Via Capponi
The attribution to Silvani is not certain, and it resembles none of his other work: with the two foreparts, joined by a balustraded terrace, the façade overlooking the street offers a very complex appearance, architecturally closer to a villa than a palazzo. The building today houses the University Department of Architecture.

154
Palazzo delle Missioni
Ca. 1640-50
Bernardino Radi
Oltrarno, Piazza Frescobaldi 1
This was the residence of the canons of the nearby church of San Jacopo. The building features an original façade in which the architect arranged a number of elements taken from the context of civil architecture: aside from the lower windows being incorporated with the openings of the mezzanine, one should note the placement of the niches and the string-course (above the first two stories).

155
Church of San Frediano in Cestello
1670-98
Pier Francesco Silvani, Giulio Cerutti and Antonio Maria Ferri
Oltrarno, Piazza del Cestello

Despite a complex and difficult period of contruction (which required the work of three different architects) the church, which was rebuilt on the foundation of a Cistercian building, is one of the most important pieces of architecture dating from baroque Florence. This is a rare case for the architecture of that period, in that it has become part of the imagery of Florence; underscored by the large and elegant tambour, this cupola dominates the skyline of Oltrarno. The plan, elongated with the central cupola, based on the sixteenth-century model; its basic outline was developed by Pier Francesco Silvani, who encountered a number of problems in execution, however. After Giulio Cerutti took over, Ferri completed the job and built the large cupola. In the final analysis, the interior is dynamic and spacious: the vertical aspect is accentuated by the eighteenth-century frescoes in the cupola.

156
Church of San Paolo Apostolo (or San Paolino)
1669-93
Giovan Battista Balatri
Quartiere Santa Maria Novella, Via Palazzuolo

This medieval church, originally owned by the Dominicans and later by the Barefoot Carmelites was rebuilt to a plan based on a Latin cross, very much like the plan of San Frediano (central cupola, greatly elongated nave and choir, arms of the transept shortened); the reproportioning of the plan completely altered its layout, in a very dignified setting, with a certain sense of space.

Florence during the Seicento

157
Church of San Giovannino degli Scolopi
1661-65
Alfonso Parigi il Giovane
Quartiere San Giovanni, Via de' Martelli
This church, property of the Jesuits beginning in 1557, was radically renovated thirteen years later by Ammannati. Parigi was assigned to redo the façade in accordance with an orthogonal framework, with niches and a tympanum, borrowing Michelangelo's motif of the recessed double columns. The church and its façade were not completed until the nineteenth century.

158
Enlargement of Palazzo Medici-Riccardi
1670-85
Pier Maria Baldi and Giovan Battista Foggini
Quartiere San Giovanni, Via Cavour 1
After this Medici palazzo (see no. 74) was sold to the marchese Gabriello Riccardi (1659), it was enlarged and renovated, beginning with the wing overlooking Via de' Ginori (this wing contains the Gallery and the Library, splendid rooms with carved panels and a frescoed and vaulted ceiling); later, following 1685, renovations were carried out in the wing overlooking Via Cavour, which contains the monumental staircase. Nowadays, it is the headquarters of the Prefecture.

159
Palazzo Orlandini del Beccuto
1679
Antonio Maria Ferri
Quartiere Santa Maria Novella, Via de' Vecchietti 6, 8
Despite the impeccable symmetry of its composition, this long façade is the product of the incorporation of two separate buildings. In the overall sobersided uniformity of its general plan, there are a few brilliant effects, such as the squared-off rustication, which is used by Ferri as a module that can be reiterated at will throughout the decorative motif that outlines the many windows in the overall elevation.

160
Corsini Chapel in the Church of the Carmine
1674-83
Pier Francesco Silvani
Oltrarno, Piazza del Carmine

In terms of size, dimension, and structure, the mausoleum dedicated to Sant'Andrea Corsini has the configuration of a separate architectural organism, simply placed alongside the structure of the church (see no. 57); this is, indeed, a space created on a central plan, enclosed amidst four triumphal arches and covered by a cupola with a lantern. Before the commission was given to Silvani, the preliminary plans had been drawn up by Pietro da Cortona.

161
Palazzo Corsini al Parione
1656-99
Antonio Maria Ferri and others
Quartiere Santa Maria Novella, Lungarno Corsini 10

This is perhaps the most important example of the civil architecture of the seventeenth century. Its design and construction involved some of the most important figures of Florentine baroque: first, the Tacca, then the Silvani (who created the spiral staircase on the interior), and finally, Ferri, who designed the monumental staircase and the cupola-covered shaft that contains it. Ferri, too, may have been behind the theatrical elevation overlooking the Arno, visually based upon the two foreparts, joined at the bottom by a long balustrade; this side presents the most efficacious image of a complex that has the size and monumental sweep worthy of a grand-ducal palace. This character was accentuated in the eighteenth century with the construction of the west wing and, above all, with the completion of the decorations on the interior. Among the most important rooms are the huge ball room and the picture gallery: a rare surviving instance of space devoted to private art collecting.

162
Villa Corsini at Castello
1698-99
Antonio Maria Ferri
Castello, Via della Pietraia
In renovating the fifteenth-century structure of this building, Ferri concentrated upon the façade of the entrance, and especially upon its central section, which was clearly designed as if it were a backdrop in a theater; he created here a vertical sequence that culminates in a tympanum joined to the roof with scrolls. The garden was created in the sixteenth century by Tribolo.

163
Palazzo dei Cartelloni
1690-93
Giovan Battista Nelli
Quartiere Santa Maria Novella, Via Sant'Antonino 11
This building, constructed for the scientist Vincenzo Viviani, is marked by a sober style of baroque architecture: it takes its name from the somewhat astonishing stone "cartelloni" (blind framed windows) that appear on the lower course of the façade. Upon them, epigraphs had been cut in honor of Galileo along with an elogy to Louis XIV, king of France.

164
Palazzo Viviani della Robbia
1693-96
Giovan Battista Foggini
Quartiere Santa Maria Novella, Via de' Tornabuoni 15
Built for a counsellor of Cosimo III, this palazzo is the only one known to have been designed by Foggini. It is a fine example of the sort of decorative exuberance that is usually reserved for religious themes. At the center of the façade is a sequence of portal, balcony, and window, continuing and underscored by a double line of undulating pediments; on the edge is a large marble escutcheon set on a double lesene.

QUARTIERE
SAN GIOVANNI

QUARTIERE
SANTA CROCE

BUILDINGS NOT IN MAP
- Oltrarno
- Quart. S. Giovanni

QUARTIERE
SANTA MARIA NOVELLA

OLTRARNO
QUARTIERE SANTO SPIRITO

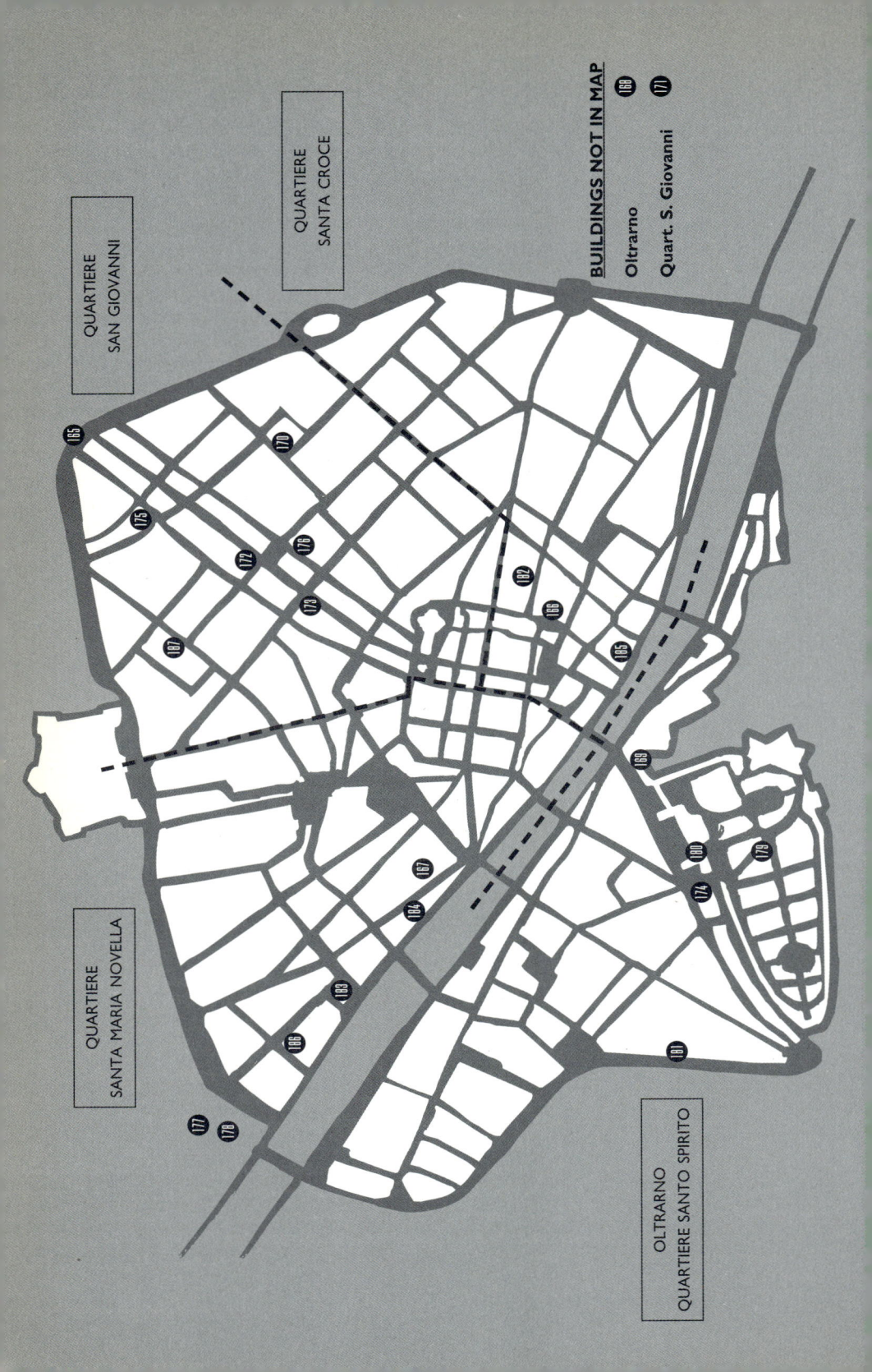

Florence under the rule of the Lorraines

Between 1740, when Florence was assigned to the Lorraines, and 1860, the year in which the city became part of the Kingdom of Italy, was a period that has traditionally been considered to be unbroken and homogeneous, despite the enormous disturbances that occurred (the Napoleonic wars, the transition to contemporary times). However slowly, the city seemed to stir and waken from the era of sloth bequeathed by the last of the Medici, slipping slowly into the climate of the age of reforms. Alongside the notion of *bello*, or beautiful, the concept of *utile* , or useful, began to make some headway, associated with a wide range of new themes: the commodities exchange, the cemetery, the customs house. A substantial portion of the holdings of the religious bodies fell under secular control, and were earmarked for institutions and structures designed for the public benefit: schools, hospitals, scientific and artistic institutions linked to the (new) concept of the museum. Through well-manned forms of neo-classicism, the architecture showed signs of responding to the new climate of reforms: Manetti, Poccianti, and Baccani are the leading figures in this new era, in which even their biographies form a uniform framework. Lest we form too simple an idea of the influences at work during this period, it should be pointed out that the last echoes of the raging battles of the Counter Reformation were just then dying out in the field of religious architecture: the great baroque façade of San Firenze was completed in 1775. Florence under the last of the Lorraines also foreshadowed some of the aspects of Florence under the rule of the Savoys: alongside the transformation of Palazzo Pitti into a royal palace, there are such major projects as the creation of the "lungarni" and the first demolition of stretches of the city walls.

165

Triumphal Arch
1738-40
Jean Nicholas Jadot
Quartiere San Giovanni, Piazza della Libertà

Hovering somewhere between the ephemeral and the eternal, this triumphal arch marked the beginning of the Age of Lorraine: indeed, it was built to salute the entrance of the grand duke Francesco Stefano of Lorraine, who arrived in Florence on 19 January 1739. The structure, designed with great simplicity and in accordance with the customary tripartite model, was then weighted down with an apparatus of decorative sculpture.

166

Church and Convent of the Filippini (or San Firenze)
1645-1775
Pier Francesco Silvani and others
Quartiere Santa Croce, Piazza San Firenze

The long, symmetrical façade of this building was built in the eighteenth century, and serves to join a number of different buildings, which had been built in the baroque style during the seventeenth and eighteenth centuries. The site of this building was that of an ancient temple originally dedicated to San Fiorenzo (over time the name was corrupted, becoming "San Firenze," a name that still applies to the entire complex). At the northern corner is the first of the two churches, with a twin façade: consecrated to Saint Filippo Neri and designed by Silvani, this church was completed in 1713 under the supervision of Gioacchino Fortini. The plan, with a single nave and with a semicircular choir, borrows a number of features from a plan that had once been set forth by Pietro da Cortona. At the opposite corner is the Oratory, built to a plan by Zanobi del Rosso in the late eighteenth century, in the form of a hall ending in a semicircle at both ends. In the center is the convent, nowadays the site of the Court of Law: this structure is arranged around a large choir, remodelled by Giovan Filippo Ciocchi in the years from 1745 to 1749, in conformity with stylistic modules that refer back to the baroque tradition.

Florence under the rule of the Lorraines

167

Former Ospedale of San Giovanni di Dio
1702-35
Carlo Marcellini
Quartiere Santa Maria Novella, Borgo Ognissanti 20
Founded at the behest of the Vespucci family in the fifteenth century, this complex was enlarged and transformed during the early eighteenth century, until it reached its current size. On that occasion, the façade overlooking the road was built, along with the church and the atrium — the latter is the most significant space in architectural terms (here, two curved staircases extend in a very theatrical manner).

168

Church of San Giorgio alla Costa (or dello Spirito Santo)
1705
Giovan Battista Foggini
Oltrarno, Via della Costa San Giorgio (near the Scuola di Sanità Militare)
This was a venerable priory, founded before the year 1000, and it was subsequently joined to the convent of Santo Spirito. The interior was later enlarged and renovated by Foggini, who welcomed the opportunity to show off his skill as a decorator: entirely adorned in white and gilt stucco, in accordance with a style that verges on the rococo, this space has a single nave, broken only by the large and lavishly decorated hanging choir.

169

Interior of the Church of Santa Felicita
1736-39
Ferdinando Ruggeri
Oltrarno, Piazza Santa Felicita
Set against the façade of this building, the Corridor by Vasari allowed direct communication with the grand-ducal residence and other buildings; it was therefore inevitable that it should be rendered a "palatine church," which Ruggieri did in a plan of remarkable monumental efficacy. Large structural forms made of "pietra serena" give a vertical momentum to the space, which is organized around a nave with chapels.

170
Palazzo Capponi
1699-1716
Carlo Fontana and others
Quartiere San Giovanni, Via Capponi 26
The large, U-shaped building was designed by Carlo Fontana in Rome, but on-site supervision was the task of Alessandro Cecchini. If the elevation overlooking the road seems to take its inspiration from the usual models of *mediocritas*, the façade facing the garden is far more complex and articulated: it is enlivened by the portico and the large windows of the far wall, as well as by two foreparts.

171
Casino della Livia
1775
Bernardo Fallani
Quartiere San Giovanni, Piazza San Marco 16
Built originally as a public office building, it was later generously given by the grand duke to the dancer Livia Malfatti Raimondi, who chose to live here. This is an early and curious example of a sixteenth-century revival: all of the decorative elements in the façade, in fact, are references to the architecture of the Buontalenti.

172
Villa at Poggio Imperiale
1767-1808
Gaspare Maria Paoletti, Pasquale Poccianti and Giuseppe Cacialli
Oltrarno, Viale di Poggio Imperiale
Formerly the suburban residence of the Salviati family, this building was expanded and transformed for the first time by Giulio Parigi (1622-24), and later by Tacca (1681-83). The present, predominantly neo-classical appearance is the result of the renovation done by Paoletti (1767-82) and Poccianti, whom together zith the Cacialli, designed the front façadem punctuated by Ionic semi-columns, and culminating in a great tympanum.

173
Biblioteca Marucelliana
1748-52
Alessandro Dori
Quartiere San Giovanni, Via Cavour 43
This institution was engendered through a bequest by the abbot, Francesco Marucelli, who died in 1703; a building was designed expressly in order to set up a public library containing his forty thousand volumes; financial assistance was also provided by the Consiglio di reggenza. Aside from all pecuniary considerations, the educational nature of the undertaking is reflected in the sober layout of the elevation.

174
Palazzo della Specola
Beginning in 1775
Giuseppe Martelli and others
Oltrarno, Via Romana 17
In the old palazzo of the Torrigiani family, a number of scientific collections were installed in the late eighteenth century; with time the collections grew, chiefly in the fields of anatomy and zoology; alongside it stands the astronomic observatory (the "specola,"), which gave its name to the entire complex. On the first floor is the Tribuna di Galileo, built in 1841 in the shape of a semicircle for the Congresso degli Scienziati.

175
Former Ospedale di Bonifacio
1787
Giuseppe Salvetti
Quartiere San Giovanni, Via San Gallo 83
This building, now the Questura, or Police Headquarters, corresponds, though only in part, to the expansion of the hospital founded in 1377 by Bonifacio Lupi (hence the name). The portico was based on the model of Santa Maria Nuova, and survives from the structure that once linked the two churches of San Luca and San Giovanni Battista, located at either end of the portico.

176

Former Ospedale di San Matteo (Accademia di Belle Arti)
Beginning in 1781
Quartiere San Giovanni, Via Ricasoli 66
The original nucleus of art collections and educational institutions was constituted by the fourteenth-century loggia of San Matteo; sealed up and remodelled, it became the site of the Accademia del Disegno. When religious and monastic organizations were suppressed, and with the acquisition of new collections, the complex came to include the former hospitals of San Matteo and San Niccolò. In 1935, the loggia was reopened.

177

Park at the Cascine
Ca. 1780-1850
Quartiere Santa Maria Novella, Piazza Vittorio Veneto
This very large park (it covers about two hundred ninety acres) grew through the progressive incorporation of farmland (the name comes from "cascine," the Italian for farmhouse) that belonged to the grand duke; the original, triangular area was wedged between the Arno and the walls of Gate of Prato. The transformation into a public garden began during the reign of Pietro Leopoldo, continuing throughout much of the reign of the Lorraines.

178

Royal Mansion at the Cascine
1787
Giuseppe Manetti
Quartiere Santa Maria Novella, Parco delle Cascine
This was the headquarters of the grand-ducal farms, and it now forms part of the great new public park; designed elegantly and built with great attention to detail, the mansion takes its inspiration from architectural models of *semplicitas*. The horizontal orientation of the front is balanced by the sequence of the portico, in which the elongated fornices alternate with the open-zork walls.

Florence under the rule of the Lorraines

179
Kaffeehaus in Boboli Gardens
1775-76
Zanobi del Rosso
Oltrarno, Boboli Gardens
A sort of architectural capriccio, located in a panoramic spot inside the park, which had by this point attained its final size and appearance. In its apparent simplicity, the volume is formed of rectilinear parts (on the uphill side) and curvilinear parts (on the downhill side): it is capped by a basket dome with a strong oriental flavor.

180
Palatine Gallery of Pitti Palace
secoli XVII-XIX
Oltrarno, Piazza Pitti
Concentrated in the north wing, the Gallery (or "Quadreria di palazzo") was opened to the public in 1828; from the seventeenth century onward, a considerable portion of the Medici and the Lorraine collections of art were housed here. With the succession of Leopold II, in 1854, began the transformation of the grand ducal apartments in the south wing, in compliance with the style of the Second Empire.

181
Torrigiani Garden
1815-21
Luigi De Cambray Digny and Gaetano Baccani
Oltrarno, Piazza Torquato Tasso
One of the most significant pieces of design in the context of Romantic style and culture. The "English style" of this garden (one of the largest in all of Florence) is here associated with a number of examples of neo-Gothic architecture; one example is the large stone tower: originally designed as an astronomical observatory, it later became a major component of the pictorial arrangement.

115

182
Palazzo Borghese
1821-22
Gaetano Baccani
Quartiere Santa Croce, Via Ghibellina 110
This small neo-classical palace was built at the order of the prince Borghese, formerly the consort of Pauline Bonaparte, after he moved to Florence: the gold and stucco, columns and mirrors on the interior made it the great meeting place of the Florentine aristocracy throughout the nineteenth century. Very little — aside from the atrium and the stairway — survives from the original seventeenth-century building designed by Gherardo Silvani.

183
Villa Favard
1857
Giuseppe Poggi
Quartiere Santa Maria Novella, Via Curtatone
One of the last, perfectly balanced expressions of the Florentine neo-classical, designed by Poggi, in a square shape, at the center of the block; in the façade overlooking the Arno, especially in the double order of columns, one can sense sixteenth-century motifs that have been filtered through an English neo-Palladianism. Nowadays, this is the department of economics of the university of Florence.

184
Palazzo Calcagnini
1857
Giuseppe Poggi
Quartiere Santa Maria Novella, Lungarno Vespucci 38
Located in the same elegant *faubourg* as Ognissanti, this building sets forth in a fairly plastic manner motifs that are similar to those found in Villa Favard, which was built about the same time (for instance, note the large arched windows); the façade, beneath the two stories that are punctuated by light lesenes, features a rusticated basement, in which the stone is perfectly, indeed impeccably shaped.

Florence under the rule of the Lorraines

185
Palazzo della Borsa, or Stock Exchange
1858-60
Michelangelo Majorfi and Emilio De Fabris
Quartiere Santa Croce, Lungarno Diaz
Part of the reorganization of the "lungarni," this building replaced the fourteenth-century complex of the Tiratoio. The entrance at the center is highlighted by the tympanum and by the Doric colonnade.
In its dignified simplicity, the façade clearly reveals the great level of adabtability to new utilitarian functions that had been incorporated into the neo-classical language.

186
Teatro Comunale, or Municipal Theater
1792-1862
Telemaco Bonaiuti and others
Quartiere Santa Maria Novella, Via Magenta
This theater was built as the "Teatro degli Intrepidi in Borgo Ognissanti," it was repeatedly remodelled, and its name was changed variously to "Arena" and to "Politeama." Radically renovated on the interior around 1960, this great building seats two thousand; with its long loggia set over the rusticated socle, the façade preserves the neo-classical appearance that it was given during the age of Lorraine.

187
Piazza Indipendenza
After 1850
Quartiere Santa Maria Novella
Situated at the heart of the new residential neighborhood of Barbano, this piazza constitutes one of the most important pieces of urban planning of the last phase of the age of Lorraine. Originally named after the princess Maria Antonia, it was later renamed when Tuscany became part of the new Italy. The handsome garden at the center of the Piazza was created later, beginning with the redesign that was started in 1869.

QUARTIERE SAN GIOVANNI

QUARTIERE SANTA CROCE

QUARTIERE SANTA MARIA NOVELLA

OLTRARNO
QUARTIERE SANTO SPIRITO

BUILDINGS NOT IN MAP
193 201
Quart. Rifredi
205
Quart. Campo di Marte

Florence during the Nineteenth and Twentieth Centuries

As brief as it may have been in historical terms, Florence's experience as the capital of Italy (1865-70) left indelible marks on the face of the city of the old regime. An engineer named Giuseppe Poggi was the leading figure in the plan that was still being implemented well beyond the year 1870; the plan which bore his name chiefly affected the outskirts of the city structure, and established a ring-road of boulevards and a sequence of piazzas along the line of the demolished walls.
Proceeding simultaneously with this project was another that struck directly at the heart of Florence: the "disembowelling" of the area of the "Mercato Vecchio," or Old Market. Upon these ruins, at the end of the century, was to rise the new office and shopping center which clustered around the piazza dedicated to Italy's first king, Victor Emanuel II.
Cosmopolitan sweep and non-provincial accents proliferated, in part due to the presence of such communities as the English expatriates; there are churches of many different confessions and persuasions, built during the last quarter of the nineteenth century. In this international atmosphere, there was also a certain weakness for antiquarian kitsch and stylistic revivals: the neo-medieval style, however, seemed to be fed by local springs. "Dantism" and references to the glories of the thirteenth and fourteenth centuries were, in many cases, the rationales behind radical renovations of buildings converted to nostalgic styles.
In the decades prior to the First World War, a Florentine version of Art Nouveau also emerged: in creations and designs that were anything but banal imitations, this school had as its most efficacious architect Giovanni Michelazzi.

188

Façade of the Church of Santa Croce
1857-63
Nicola Matas
Quartiere Santa Croce, Piazza Santa Croce
The long-debated matter of the façade of this church (see no. 35) found its solution in one of the many models developed by Matas between 1837 and 1857; the choice fell at that point upon a tricuspidal solution that was moderately medieval in style, hearkening back to the Florentine polychrome tradition. Closer to the models created by Arnolfo was the bell tower, which was designed by Baccani and completed in 1865.

189

Royal Suite of Apartments in the Pitti Palace
18th-19th century
Oltrarno, Piazza Pitti
The house of Savoia completed the decoration of this palace, decoration which had been begun under the house of Lorraine: in the apartments located in the south wing, drapery, mirrors, and gilding created the atmosphere of a great palace (see no. 180). From 1919 onward, the museum took over the entire building, joining galleries and royal apartments in an inextricable whole that seems to be articulated in a time-space sequence of decorated rooms.

190

Covered Marketplace of San Lorenzo
1869-74
Giuseppe Mengoni
Quartiere San Giovanni, Via dell'Ariento
The architect of the Galleria of Milan showed here that he was able to join a traditional architectural language with a building structure that used forward-looking techniques and materials; above the masonry socle, shaped in accordance with classical modules, rises the structure made of glass and castiron, reminiscent of international models.

191
Façade of the Church of Santa Maria del Fiore
1876-87
Emilio De Fabris and Luigi Del Moro
Quartiere San Giovanni, Piazza San Giovanni
After a first (1859) and a second competition (1865), neither of which resulted in a winning design, the neo-Gothic plan by De Fabris was chosen in 1867; that plan was linked stylistically with Giotto's bell tower (see no. 36, 37). In the final design, however, the tricuspidal crowning — similar to the one on Santa Croce — was eliminated in favor of a "basilican" solution proposed by Luigi Del Moro.

192
Palazzo Serristori
1873
Mariano Falcini
Oltrarno, Lungarno Serristori, corner of Piazza Demidoff
The nineteenth-century renovation of this building coincided with the opening of the "lungarno" (1869); behind the sober-sided façade, with a high rusticated basement, stands the atrium that reveals the original sixteenth-century form (one should note, for example, the triple Venetian window). In the last quarter of the nineteenth century, the interiors were completed renovated in "eighteenth-century style," with gilding, stuccos, and large hanging mirrors.

193
"Tepidarium" Greenhouse
1879-80
Giacomo Roster
Quartiere Rifredi, Via Bolognese, corner of Via XX Settembre
This is a brilliant piece of architecture in iron and glass, prepared within the boundaries of the Garden of the Pellegrino, on the occasion of the first National Exposition of Horticulture. Made with prefabricated centering, pillars, and prefabricated beams, the building followed the many examples produced outside of Italy (in particular, the great greenhouse at Kew Gardens, in London).

194
Piazza d'Azeglio
1862-66
Quartiere Santa Croce
Even though this piazza dates from prior to Florence's brief stint as Italy's capital, it appears more "Piemontese" than any of the other piazzas built in the nineteenth century. Practically the eastern counterweight to the Piazza Indipendenza, the buildings that surround the rectangular space were built by the Società Anonima Edificatrice, in part on the land of Villa Ginori.

195
Piazza Beccaria
1865-77
Giuseppe Poggi and Giacomo Roster
Quartiere Santa Croce
This was the first piazza built along the new ring of boulevards; the isolation of the Gate of Santa Croce became an opportunity to design various segments of a uniform backdrop, arranged in a ring around the new urban space. Poggi conceived the buildings, with rusticated socle and lesenes in a giant order, in a distinctly classical manner that we will find elsewhere as well.

196
Piazza Cavour (now Piazza Libertà)
1865-73
Giuseppe Poggi and Giacomo Roster
Quartiere San Giovanni
The four large exterior blocks are unified by their "Tuscan style," which is especially distinctive in the continuous loggia. The area occupied by the piazza, thus marked out, is far larger than was customary, and contains not only the "isolated" gate (see no. 28): therefore, a special design was required; Poggi conceived it as an oval garden with a basin in the center.

Florence during the Nineteenth and Twentieth Centuries

197

Piazza della Mulina (now Piazza Poggi)
1865-76
Giuseppe Poggi and N. Frosali
Oltrarno, Lungarno Cellini
The idea of the piazza, engendered by the isolation of a venerable city gate (see no. 42), was developed into an alternative approach through the slope that serves as a backdrop here. The space was meant to be symmetrical, surrounded by four small buildings with extreme rustication; the two that were built, in any case, beckon one toward the monumental ramps that lead to the Piazzale Michelangelo.

198

Viale dei Colli and Piazzale Michelangelo
1871-76
Giuseppe Poggi
Oltrarno, Viale Galileo and Viale Machiavelli
On the hills of the Oltrarno, between Porta Romana and Porta San Niccolò, Poggi's plan was completed with a painterly sequence of boulevards. Linked to the concept of the panorama was this piazzale, located between the hill of San Miniato and the Lungarno; the square is consecrated to the memory of Michelangelo, with copies of some of his most famous works on display in the square (the *David* is shown here) and in the loggia, which was later transformed into a cafe.

199

Piazza Vittorio Emanuele (now Piazza della Repubblica)
1883-96
Vincenzo Micheli and others
Quartiere Santa Maria Novella and Quartiere Santa Croce
The decision to construct the piazza was made as early as 1866, and the necessary demolition and reconstruction covers a vast surface area, corresponding to the center of the Roman *castrum* (the Forum), and later to the area of the Mercato Vecchio and the Jewish Ghetto. Around the circumference of the piazza, stylistically homogeneous but not uniform, stands the great triumphal arch, set on an axis with the Via Strozzi.

200
Palazzo and Museo Bardini
Ca. 1890-1910
Stefano Bardini
Oltrarno, Piazza de' Mozzi
This institution was created in 1923 through a bequest by Stefano Bardini, an antiquarian and art collector; in the decorous neo-classical palazzo is a vast array of tapestries, porcelains, paintings, sculptures, and archeological finds that range from ancient times to the eighteenth century. There are also a great many items, such as the two altars walled into the façade, which come from buildings that had been demolished.

201
Villa Stibbert
1880-88
Gaetano Fortini
Quartiere Rifredi, Via Stibbert 26
In his trasformation of the villa and the estate that once belonged to the Davanzati family, the wealthy English art collector Frederick Stibbert incorporated an astonishing array of diverse stylistic references, summing up in a limited space an enormous repertory of kitsch: it ranges from the neo-Gothic towers to the neo-sixteenth-century elevation, from the little Neo-Egyptian temple to the Palladian rotunda.

202
Building of the Woolworkers' Guild, or Palazzo dell'Arte della Lana
14th century, rebuilt in 1905
Enrico Lusini
Quartiere Santa Croce, Via di Calimala, corner of Via dell'Arte della Lana
This is the finest example of a late Romantic restatement of fourteenth-century architecture. The building, known as "il Torrione," (the keep) once belonged to the Campiobbesi family. It was purchased by the Società Dantesca and radically remodelled, incorporating among other things items that were brought in from elsewhere, such as the corner tabernacle. The façade overlooking the Via Calimala, on the other hand, is original.

203

Villa Bardini (or Torre del Gallo)
Ca. 1900
Stefano Bardini
Oltrarno, Via della Costa San Giorgio 2-6,
With its great park, the estate extends all the way to the foot of the hill, nearly merging physically with the Palazzo Bardini. This neo-Gothic villa is the suburban appendage to the palazzo and the art collections; in a picturesque setting, but with the same antiquarian style, a similar collection of architectural fragments has been set up here.

204

Alighieri Family Home
1875-1910
Giuseppe Castellucci and others
Quartiere Santa Croce, Via Santa Margherita corner of Via Alighieri
This is a piece of architecture closely linked to "Dantism," a late Romantic school of Italian culture that involved the discovery (or invention} of places linked to the life of the great poet. This is believed to be the house in which Dante Alighieri was born, offering an opportunity to recreate a "typically thirteenth-century setting," focusing on the museum-home and the collection of memorabilia of Dante.

205

Church of the Sette Santi Fondatori
1901-10
Luigi Caldini
Quartiere Campo di Marte, Viale dei Mille
Although it is based on a plan of the most traditional sort, this church constitutes one of the highest forms of expression of the Florentine neo-Gothic; the references to the Middle Ages appear in a contaminated version here, not too different from the buildings constructed around the same time, for a synagogue and a Greek-Orthodox church.

206
Russian Orthodox Church
1899-1903
Michail Preobragenski and others
Quartiere Rifredi, Viale Milton, corner of Via Leone X

Together with the Episcopalian and Anglican churches, this building consecrated to the Russian-Orthodox religion was a perfect expression of the cosmopolitan culture of Florence. Closely based on traditional models, the design was developed in Russia, and entrusted to Florentine architects and craftsmen, who reinterpreted the Russian and Byzantine iconography in certain details.

207
Carnielo Home and Studio
1911-12
Rinaldo Carnielo (?)
Quartiere Campo di Marte, Piazza Savonarola 14

This building today contains the offices of a foundation dedicated to the sculptor Rinaldo Carnielo, who lived here, worked here, and in all likelihood, designed its unusual façade. Some consider this to be a piece of Florentine Liberty, the Italian equivalent of Art Nouveau, while others consider it to be an example of "secession" architecture. In any case, it is difficult categorize it stylistically, and it was certainly the work of an original and fertile mind.

208
Vichi Home and Gallery
1911
Giovanni Michelazzi
Quartiere Santa Maria Novella, Borgo Ognissanti 26

This may well be the most significant project of Florentine Art Nouveau, despite the narrow space it occupies (a vertical slice of a building): it made use of a curving framework, to which were adroitly linked a number of whimsical decorative elements, thus enlarging and enriching the façade, giving an organic continuity to the two vertical portions (gallery and residence).

209
Jewish Synagogue
1874-82
Vincenzo Micheli
Quartiere Santa Croce, Via Farini 4
Here as elsewhere in Unified Italy, the building was the result of the activisim of the Jewish community and the new climate of official tolerance; unlike the synagogues of Turin or Rome, alongside the usual eastern decorative repertory (Moorish, Byzantine, Egyptian) there is an effort to reach out to the local tradition, present here in the form of a two-tone marble facing.

210
Main Building of the Central National Library
1911-35
Cesare Bazzani
Quartiere Santa Croce, Piazza Cavalleggeri
This is an institution that dates from when Florence was the capital of Italy, and it remained here even after the government moved to Rome. The core of the collection was the Fondo Magliabechi (1714), which grew over the course of the nineteenth and twentieth centuries. The modern building includes a part of the monastery of Santa Croce; designed for a national competition (1902), its strongest feature is the elaborate and original terracotta façade.

211
Villino Broggi
1910-11
Giovanni Michelazzi
Quartiere Campo di Marte, Via Scipione Ammirato 99
The sheer plastic skill of Michelazzi here encountered a volume, and no longer a two-dimensional surface; the result is an unusual degree of correspondence between exterior shell and interior arrangment of space, all organized around a spiral staircase. Decorations and furnishings, which are still intact, completed the design.

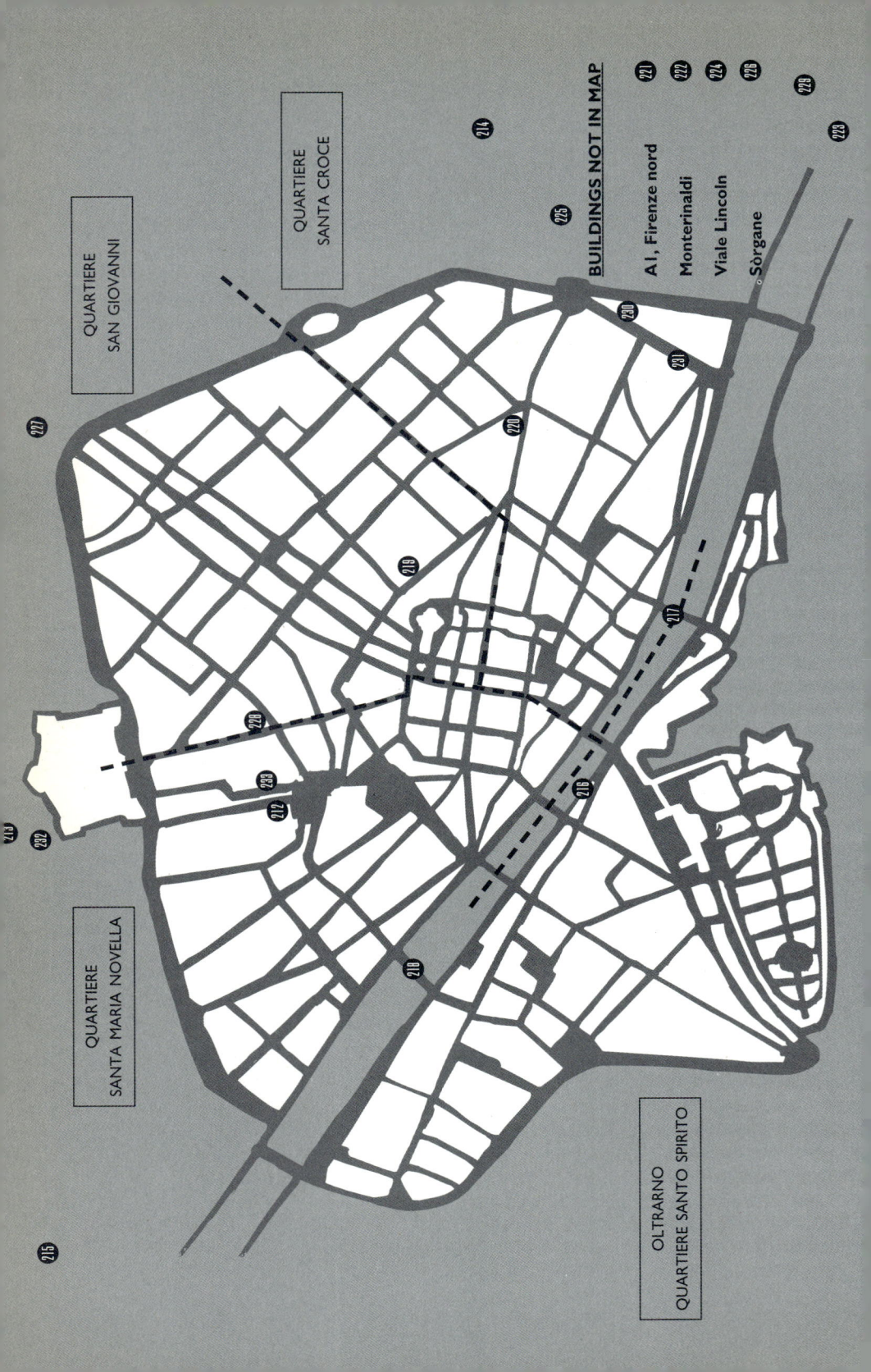

QUARTIERE
SAN GIOVANNI

QUARTIERE
SANTA CROCE

BUILDINGS NOT IN MAP

221
222 A1, Firenze nord
224 Monterinaldi
226 Viale Lincoln
228 Sorgane
223

QUARTIERE
SANTA MARIA NOVELLA

OLTRARNO
QUARTIERE SANTO SPIRITO

Florence and Modern Architecture

The burden of an ever-present past does not hinder a certain number of the architects working in Florence from following the most radical modern schools of architectural thought . Stadiums and railroad stations are among the most important works of architecture in Italy during this period, in a display of intellectual effervescence that may be somehow related to the flourishing literary climate in Florence between the two world wars. If the stadium built by Pierluigi Nervi constitutes a case that is quite "sui generis," quite to the contrary, the railroad station — the work of a number of "young" architects who were destined to become "masters" — paradoxically enough hints at a possible link with tradition (through a continuity of materials, not necessarily of forms). In so alluding, we are thinking more of Giovanni Michelucci than of Italo Gamberini, with reference to the two most important figures in the so-called "Tuscan Group."

The following generation, which came to the profession during the Second World War (among them, Detti, Ricci, Savioli), found themselves facing the challenges of the place that surrounded them: some with environmental values, such as was case with Monterinaldi, but chiefly with the overwhelming heritage of art and history. In Florence especially this area of exploration forces one to consider the relationship between the city and its river, by focusing on the matter of the bridge (which at times involves a reconstruction of façades). Beneath the eyes of a well informed public opinion, we shall see a wide ranges of zays of dealing with the issue, ranging from the Ponte Vecchio, "redone exactly as it was," right on down to the matter of structural performance of the Ponte Vespucci and the Ponte all'Indiano.

212
Railroad Station of Santa Maria Novella
1932-34
Italo Gamberini, Giovanni Michelucci and others
Quartiere Santa Maria Novella, Piazza della Stazione

This building is a symbol of Florence during the Thirties, and is one of the most signficant works, in all of Italy, of the new architecture. Following a competition in 1932, the commission was assigned to the young architects of the "Tuscan Group," and not without considerable controversy: among them was Gamberini, who had developed a sort of preliminary project for his final university examination. The complex interaction with the existing Gothic structures was here cushioned by the stone covering, but it was chiefly channeled through an elementary language based on the juxtaposition of large volumes. The functional organization appears perfectly joined to the surrounding street grid, and in particular, in terms of the problem of the entrances, diversified also because of the differences in level. On the interior is the passenger gallery, running perpendicular to the tracks, and constituting the fulcrum of the structural system of distribution: all of the functions intended to serve the public converge on this space, which is emphasized by the great glass roof.

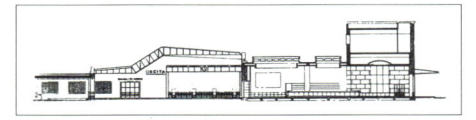

213
Railroad Buildings
1929-34
Angiolo Mazzoni
Quartiere Rifredi, Via delle Ghiacciaie 2 and Via Cittadella 40

These structures were ancillary to the construction of the building serving passengers, and they were designed from 1929 on: the first of these buidlings was the post office building located in the Via Alamanni; the next to be built was the complex structure of the heating plant which, more than the others, displays signs of the Constructivist style of Angiolo Mazzoni. In 1934, last of all, came the building for the track and railyard workers.

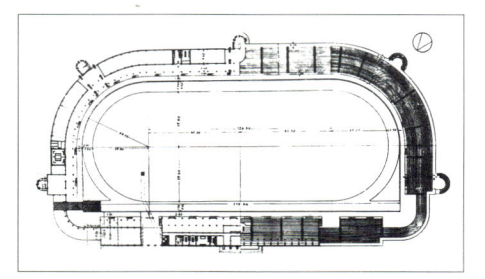

Florence and Modern Architecture

214
City Stadium
1929-32
Pier Luigi Nervi
Quartiere Campo di Marte, Viale Manfredo Fanti 4/4

This structure, built entirely in visible reinforced concrete, stands in the former "campo di Marte"; intended for track and field, as well as soccer, this stadium was built in two phases, following a competition, in which Nervi acted as a developer. The need to reduce costs resulted in the uniform cross-section of the interior of the stadium, with a regular sequence of cement pillars, with a regular sequence of cement pillars supporting the intrados of the bleachers. In the context of this uniform structure, a few features stand out as "architectural" exceptions: the the canopy structure, made up of twenty-four large brackets made of reinforced concrete; the extremely aerodynamic tower bearing the flagstaff, called the tower of Marathon, stands seventy meters high. Twisting around its base is the spiral ramp that leads from the ground floor to the upper edge of the grandstand. Built partly in preparation for the world soccer championships in 1934, it was then radically renovated on the occasion of the world cup games of 1990.

215
Cinema and Theater Puccini
1939-40
Technichal office of the State Division of Market Monopolies
Quartiere Rifredi, Piazza Puccini

This building was initially planned for the recreational center for workers in the Tobacco Processing and Manufacturing Division. Though it is based on an extremely simple conception, it is one of the finest and most efficacious pieces of architecture for leisure time of the entire Fascist era. The composition, clearly horizontal in orientation, is given great upward thrust by the glassed-in tower that contains a winding staircase.

216
Buildings along the Arno near the Ponte Vecchio
Beginning in 1950
Italo Gamberini and the city planning offices
Oltrarno, Borgo San Jacopo and Via de' Bardi

After the widespread devastation caused by the Second World War, the comptetion and the debate which followed, strained, to the utmost limit, the skills and patience of the city's architects, split innovators and traditionalists: on the south bank of the Arno (where the buildings overlook the water directly) a compromise was finally reached between the "modern" language of the façades and the traditional volumetric arrangement.

217
Ponte alle Grazie
1946-53
Giovanni Michelucci, Edoardo Detti and others
Between the Lungarno delle Grazie and Lungarno Serristori

This corresponds to one of Florence's three historic bridges; it existed as early as the thirteenth century, and it was destroyed in August 1944. Like the Ponte alla Carraia, this bridge too was the subject in 1946 of a creative competition: the winning design, featuring four tall and slender piers, was partly the work of Riccardo Gizdulich, who was in charge of reconstruction of the Ponte di Santa Trinita.

218
Ponte Vespucci
1954-57
Riccardo Morandi and others
Between the Lungarno Vespucci and Lungarno Soderini

In this instance, the bridge is not a reconstruction; it was in fact built *ex-novo*. As he had done in other projects, here Riccardo Morandi was striving for structural lightness, obtained through the reduction of bulk and weight of the platband, or flat arch, wich supports the roadway: the final effect is that of a single, slightly curved span.

219

Main Office Building of the Cassa di Risparmio, or Savings Bank
1953-57
Giovanni Michelucci
Quartiere San Giovanni, Via Bufalini 6
This building is made up of two rectangular structures, adjoining and slightly offset. The simplest of the two structures is the office building, while the more complex one contains the main hall, covered by a sequence of vaults running perpendicular to the façade. From this volumetric design emerge two radically different elevations, one on the front and one on the back.

220

Building of the Provincial Headquarters of the Mail and Telegraph Service
1959-67
Giovanni Michelucci
Quartiere Santa Croce, Via Pietrapiana 53-55
The arrangement of the structure has the shape of a U, arranyed around an interior road, and according to a double vertical order, corresponding to the main hall for the public. On the exterior, the great volume appears to be punctuated by the window modules; simple as it is, it is focused by the contrast between the background of hewn stone and the jutting sections made of bare cement.

221

Church of San Giovanni Battista (or dell'Autostrada)
1960-64
Giovanni Michelucci
Autostrada del Sole, near the exit Firenze-N
Many consider this to be the emblematic building, summing up perfectly the poetics of Michelucci. It is a building of great volumetric complexity, designed as if it were a great sculpture. The "tent," in terms of elevation, and the "cross," in terms of plan, are the two driving elements of inspiration for the architect: the rustication of the stone basement creates an intentional clash with the copper surface of the large "gores" of the roof.

222

Residential Complex at Monterinaldi
1952-62
Leonardo Ricci and others
Monterinaldi, Via Bolognese
First, Casa Ricci, and later, Casa Petrelli, constituted the first nucleus of a group of single-family homes located amidst rocks and trees along a panoramic ridge to the north of Florence. An *organic* relationship with the environment determined a number of the architectural characteristics, which are evident both in the casing material, and in the layout of the plan.

223

Ponte da Verrazzano
1967-69
Leonardo Savioli and others
Between the Lungarno Ferrucci and Lungarno Cristoforo Colombo
Situated to the east of the city, in a zone of expansion, this building too was the result of a creative competition: it is formed by two large projecting brackets, linked by a central beam, extending over an overall distance or span of one hundred fifteen meters. Foot traffic over this bridge is separated from automobile traffic.

224

Ponte all'Indiano
1969-76
Fabrizio De Miranda, Paolo Sica and Adriano Montemagni
Between Viale Lincoln and Lungarno dei Pioppi
Standing at the edge of the city, in a zone to the west, behind the Park at the Cascine (where the Tomba dell'Indiano that gives the bridge its name is located). The system of engineering that was used here is a single span (two hundred ten meters in length) supported, with a series of steel tie-rods, by two large lateral piers: on this bridge, too, foot traffic runs over a catwalk that is separate from automobile traffic.

Florence and Modern Architecture

225
Residential Building in the Via Piagentina
1964-67
Leonardo Savioli and Danilo Santi
Quartiere Campo di Marte, Via Piagentina 29

The many problems of the corner house are solved here with a plan of exceeding spatial complexity. As in other buildings by Savioli, this one appears to be dominated by a plastic approach to architecture: a sort of *New Brutalism* "alla fiorentina," in which the bare reinforced-concrete surfaces are continually cut by sculptural elements that display a (false) modular layout.

226
Neighborhood of Public Housing at Sòrgane
1962-80
Leonardo Ricci, Leonardo Savioli and others
Village of Sòrgane, Bagno a Ripoli

This, together with the neighborhood of the Isolotto, constitutes the largest public works project (GESCAL and INCIS were the agencies) in the postwar period. Entrusted to two teams of architects (one supervised by Ricci, the other by Savioli), the residences are designed with a series of linear features, punctuated by horizontal walkways: among these buildings is the best known one in the complex, known as "La Nave," or The Ship, and built in 1962-68.

227
Headquarters of "Nuova Italia" (now IBM)
1968-72
Edoardo Detti
Quartiere Campo di Marte, Via Giacomini 8

In its open avowal of simplicity, this building — constructed for one of the most respected publishing houses in Italy — represents one of the trends that was then predominant; the final design was in part the work of Carlo Scarpa, and called for two counterpoised structures, enclosing an *hortus conclusus*, or inner garden. The crown of the building features elements that link the two structures.

228
Building of BICA in the Via Nazionale
1957
Italo Gamberini
Quartiere Santa Maria Novella, Via Nazionale 87
Set in a continuous grid of construction, this office building concentrates in the façade its most remarkble features; it was conceived as a uniform sequence of glass modules and horizontal strips of masonry. The metal grids of the movable *brise-soleils*, and the arrangement of the crowning cantilever roof, confer a remarkable lightness to this building.

229
Regional Headquarters of RAI-TV
1962-68
Italo Gamberini
Quartiere Campo di Marte, Lungarno Colombo, Largo De Gasperi 1
A poetics of functionality distinguishes this building, based on complex concepts of distribution. Particularly evident in the volumetric conceptions, the block of vertical connections constitutes the linking element between the two building blocks, separate and respectively orthogonal, which make up the entire structure.

230
Headquarters of the State Archives
1972-88
Italo Gamberini and others
Quartiere Santa Croce, Viale Amendola and Viale Giovane Italia
Designed following a competition in 1971, this massive building fit in with the pentagonal shape of the lot, which lies between the river Arno and the Piazza Beccaria. In the eastern wing, with jutting steps, the records are stored (once housed in the Uffizi); a large internal road divides this section from the western part, with offices and workshops.

231
Office Building of "La Nazione"
1961-66
Pier Luigi Spadolini
Quartiere Santa Croce, Viale Giovane Italia 4
Here too we find ourselves looking at a large-scale complex, broken down into a series of volumes, intended for different functions. Here, as in the later designs, Spadolini repeats and inserts standard, prefabricated modules into the façades.

232
Residential Building in Piazza San Jacopino
1973-76
Marco Dezzi Bardeschi
Quartiere Rifredi, Piazza San Jacopino
The design of an apartment building is here translated into a complex interplay of intersections between prisms and cylinders, in accordance with a plastic vision of volume. In its provocative conception, this building rejects the "vocation for dialogue" which is so common in a great deal of Florentine architecture, through adaptations to the shape of the lot, volumetric analogies, and affinities of material.

233
Bus Terminal
1987-90
Cristiano Toraldo di Francia
Quartiere Santa Maria Novella, Via Valfonda
This structure is one of the new infrastructures that surround the train station of Santa Maria Novella. In this case, the long cantilever roof, which constitutes the heart of the project, is preceded by cylindrical volumes; above all, these elements, which are covered in two-tone marble strips, distinguish the architecture of the bus terminal.

Glossary

Acroterium
A pedestal placed upon a pediment - at each base, or at the apex - to support a statue, or other ornamentation.

Apse
A vaulted semicircular or polygonal recess in a building, especially at the eastern end of the choir of a church, and at either end of the transept.

Arcade
A series of arches supported on piers or columns, open or closed at the back.

Ashlar
A hewn or squared building stone, permitting very thin masonry joints.

Attic
A low story or decorative wall above an entablature or the main cornice of a building.

Balustrade
A railing with supporting balusters, serving as an open parapet (as along the edge of a balcony, terrace, bridge, staircase, or the eaves of a building).

Basilica
An early Christian church building, consisting of a high nave, two or four side aisles with clerestory, a semicircular apse, and sometimes a narthex.

Composite capital - Composite order
Belonging to or being a modification of the Corinthian order introduced in Roman imperial times by combining angular Ionic volutes with the acanthus-circled bell of the Corinthian.

Corbel
An architectural member which projects from within a wall and supports a superincumbent weight; especially one that is stepped upward from a vertical surface.

Corbeled window
Window with a corbeled projection supporting its external sill.

Cornice
The typically molded and projecting horizontal member that crowns an architectural composition; specifically, the uppermost of the three members of a classical entablature.

Drum, or **Tambour**
A circular wall (as one supporting a dome).

Exedra
A permanent outdoor bench, nearly semicircular, with high, solid back.

Lantern
A structure with glazed or open sides raised above an opening in a roof to light or ventilate an enclosed space below.

Loggia
A roofed open gallery or arcade in the side of a building, especially when facing upon an open court; also, such a gallery or arcade set at the height of one or more stories and not projecting from the surface of the building but forming an integral part of the building.

Oculus
An architectural member resembling or suggesting an eye; a small round window.

Pendentive
Any of several spandrels, in the form of spherical triangles, forming a transition between the circular plan of a dome and the polygonal plan of the supporting masonry.

Peristyle
A colonnade surrounding a building or an open space, specifically, a range of roof-supporting columns with their entablature on all sides of a building or an inner court.

Pier
A square pillar; any support of masonry or the like for sustaining vertical pressure.

Pilotis
A column of iron, steel, or reinforced concrete supporting a building above an open ground level.

Pilaster
An upright architectural member

138

that is rectangular in plan and is structurally a pier but architecturally treated as a column, that with capital, shaft, and base usually projects one third of its width or less from the wall, and that may be load-bearing or merely applied as a surface decoration.

Pinnacle
A relatively small, upright structure, commonly terminating in a gable, a pyramid or a cone, rising above the roof or coping of a building, or capping a tower, buttress, or other projecting architectural member.

Portico
A structure consisting of a roof supported by columns or piers, usually attached to a building as a porch.

Presbytery
The part of a church (as the choir or sanctuary or both) reserved for the officiating clergy.

Pronaos
The outer part of an ancient Greek temple forming a portico immediately in front of the cella and delimited by the front wall of the cella and the columns or the antae and columns, also, the narthex of an early church.

Scarsella
Special type of apse of a building, especially a church, usually built to a central plan.

Tympanum
The recessed, usually triangular space enclosed between the horizontal and sloping cornices of a pediment, often decorated with sculpture.

Trefoil
An ornament or symbol in the form of a stylized trifoliolate leaf; especially, a three-lobed foliation in Gothic tracery.

Tribune
The bishop's throne in a basilican church or the apsidal structure containing it; an apsidal structure in a public building (as an Italian church).

Tricuspidate façade
Façade crowned with three cusps, commonly found in Gothic churches.

Venetian window
An architectural unit consisting of a central window with an arched head and on each side a usually narrower window with a square head.

Vestibule
A passage, hall, or antechamber between the outer door and the interior parts of a house or a building.

Volute
A spiral, scroll-shaped ornament that forms the chief feature of the Ionic capital and that also appears in the Corinthian and Composite capitals.

Index of places

The names in small capital letters refer to those buildings covered at lenghth in this guide book.
The **boldface** numbers refer to the numbering of the files, not the page number.

A
ABBEY OF FIESOLE **10**, **81**, 29
ABBEY OF FLORENCE **8**, 35
 ABBEY OF FLORENCE, CHIOSTRO DEGLI ARANCI **61**
ABBEY OF SAN SALVATORE **7**
Accademia del Disegno 114
Accademia Platonica 68
ALIGHIERI FAMILY HOME **204**
Arena (Municipal Theater) 117

B
BARGELLO (OR PALAZZO DEL POPOLO) **31**, 39, 42
Basilica di Santa Reparata 44
BAPTISTERY OF SAN GIOVANNI **12**, 9, 29, 30, 32, 75
BIBLIOTECA LAURENZIANA (OR LAURENTIAN LIBRARY) **111**, 15
Biblioteca Medicea 11
BIBLIOTECA MARUCELLIANA **173**
BOBOLI GARDENS **121**, 72, 89, 94
BRIDGES
 ALL'INDIANO **224**, 129
 alla Carraia 132
 ALLE GRAZIE **217**
 DA VERRAZZANO **223**
 di San Niccolò 20
 OF SANTA TRINITA **134**, 132
 VESPUCCI **218**, 129
BUILDING OF THE PROVINCIAL HEADQUARTERS OF THE MAIL AND TELEGRAPH SERVICE **220**

BUILDINGS ALONG THE ARNO NEAR PONTEVECCHIO **216**
BUS TERMINAL **233**

C
Campo di Marte 131
CARNIELO HOME AND STUDIO **207**
Casa Petrelli 134
Casa Ricci 134
CASINO DELLA LIVIA **171**
Castello di Altafronte 50
CHARTERHOUSE OF GALLUZZO (OR OF FLORENCE) **46**, 49
CHURCHES
CARMINE, CORSINI CHAPEL **160**, 106
FILIPPINI (OR SAN FIRENZE) **166**, 109, 110
MADONNA DE' RICCI **141**
OGNISSANTI **143**
SAN CARLO DEI LOMBARDI **41**
SAN DOMENICO IN FIESOLE **77**
SAN FELICE IN PIAZZA **70**
SAN FRANCESCO IN FIESOLE **45**
SAN FREDIANO IN CESTELLO **155**
SAN GIORGIO ALLA COSTA (OR DELLO SPIRITO SANTO) **168**
SAN GIOVANNI BATTISTA (OR DELL'AUTOSTRADA) **221**
San Giovanni Battista 113
SAN GIOVANNINO DEGLI SCOLOPI **157**
SAN GIOVANNINO DEI CAVALIERI **97**
SAN GIUSEPPE **96**
SAN JACOPO IN CAMPO CORBOLINI 20

SAN JACOPO SOPR'ARNO **19**, 103
SAN LORENZO **65**, 9, 11, 49, 60, 62, 65, 99, 100
SAN LORENZO, CHAPEL OF THE PRINCES **144**, 11, 97, 99
San Luca 113
SAN MARCO **76**, 15, 55, 67
San Michele (demolished) 32
SAN MICHELE A SAN SALVI **18**
SAN MINIATO AL MONTE **11**, 29, 32
SAN NICCOLÒ SOPR'ARNO **59**
SAN PAOLO APOSTOLO (OR SAN PAOLINO) **156**
SAN REMIGIO **21**
SAN SALVATORE AL MONTE (OR SAN FRANCESCO AL MONTE) **95**
SAN SALVATORE AL VESCOVO **15**
SANT'AMBROGIO **58**
Sant'Egidio 101
SANTA CROCE **35**, 27, 41, 46, 121
SANTA CROCE, CHAPEL OF THE PAZZI **69**
SANTA CROCE, GREAT CLOISTER **69**
SANTA CROCE, FAÇADE **188**
SANTA FELICITA (INTERIOR) **169**, 88
SANTA FELICITA, BARBADORI CHAPEL **66**
Santa Maria degli Angeli 67
SANTA MARIA DEL CARMINE **57**

141

Index of places

Santa Maria del Fiore **36**, **191**, 9, 11, 12, 25, 27, 31, 41, 43, 44, 45, 50, 55, 93, 100
Santa Maria del Fiore, Belltower (or Giotto's Belltower) **37**, 121
Santa Maria del Fiore, Dome **62**, 10, 12
Santa Maria del Fiore, Façade **191**
Santa Maria delle Vigne 46
Santa Maria Maddalena de' Pazzi (or Cestello) **91**
Santa Maria Maggiore **16**
Santa Maria Novella **39**, **85**, 27, 41, 47
Santa Maria Novella, Façade **85**
Santa Maria Nuova 113
Santa Reparata (Ruins) **6**, **31**, **44**
Santa Trinita **40**, **135**, 41, 43, 46
Santa Trinita, Façade **135**
Santi Apostoli **14**
Santi Michele e Gaetano **142**
Santi Simone e Giuda **145**
Santissima Annunziata **78**, **140**, 55, 100
Santissima Annunziata, Coloredo Chapel 98
Santissima Annunziata, Chapel of Saint Sebastian 98
Santissima Annunziata, Feroni Chapel 98
Santo Spirito **68**, 9, 79
Santo Stefano al Ponte **17**
Santo Stefano al Ponte (interior) **146**
Russian Ortodox **206**
Sette santi fondatori **205**
Teatini 99
Chiostrino dei voti 67
Chiostro verde 46
Cinema and Theater Puccini **215**
City Stadium **214**
Cloister of San Domenico 66
Cloister of Sant'Antonino 66
Cloister of the Scalzo **98**
Complex of the Tiratoio 117
Convents
   de la Tourette 49

Filippini (or San Firenze) **166**
Santissima Annunziata **78**, **140**, 100
San Domenico in Fiesole **77**
San Marco **76**, 67
Santa Croce **35**
Santa Maria Novella **39**, 27, 41, 47
Santa Maria Novella, (cloister), Cappellone degli Spagnoli 46
Santo Spirito 111
Covered Marketplace of San Lorenzo **190**

F

Fiesole
   Archeological area **1**, 24, 25
   Cathedral **9**
   Theater **3**
   Ruins of the temple **2**
   Ruins of the Baths **4**
Former Church of San Pancrazio (Rucellai Chapel and Marini Museum) **56**
Former Ospedale di Bonifacio **175**
Former Ospedale di San Giovanni di Dio **167**
Former Ospedale di San Matteo (Accademia di Belle Arti) **176**, 114
Former Ospedale di San Niccolò 114
Forte Belvedere (or the Fort of San Giorgio) **136**, 19
Fortezza da Basso (or St. John the Baptist Fortress) **112**

G

Galleria Vittorio Emanuele (Milan) 120
Galluzzo 52
Garden of the Pellegrino 121
Gates
   of Prato **29**, 114
   San Gallo **28**, 37
   Faenza 84
   Romana **43**, 123
   San Frediano (or porta Pisana, or porta Carraia) **44**, 48
   San Niccolò **42**, 123
   Santa Croce 122

H

Headquarters of the Società Dante Alighieri 52
Headquarters of "Nuova Italia" (now IBM) **227**
Headquarters of the State Archives **230**
Hill of Montaguto 49
Hill of San Francesco 24
Hill of Sant'Apollinare 24
Hospital of Santa Maria Nuova **147**
House of Bianca Cappello **125**

J

Jewish Ghetto 123
Jewish synagogue **209**

K

Kaffeehaus in Boboli Gardens **179**
Kew Gardens 121

L

Library of Palazzo Medici-Riccardi 105
Logge
   Bigallo **38**
   Mercato Nuovo **114**
   Pesce **115**
   Rucellai **83**
   San Matteo 114
   San Paolo **92**
   Signoria (or dei Lanzi, or dell'Orcagna) **55**, 10, 21, 53

M

Main Building of the Central National Library **210**
Main Office Building of the Cassa di Risparmio, or Saving Bank **219**
Medici Casino **126**
Monastery and Refectory of Santa Apollonia **60**
Monastery of Santa Croce 127
Museo Bardini **200**
Museo Marino Marini (Former Church of San Pancrazio) **56**
Museum of the History of Science 50

Index of places

N
NEIGHBORHOOD OF PUBLIC HOUSING AT SÒRGANE (THE "NAVE") **226**
Notarial Archives 52

O
OFFICE BUILDING OF "LA NAZIONE" **231**
ORSANMICHELE (OR CHURCH OF SAN MICHELE IN ORTO) **51**, 51
OSPEDALE DEGLI INNOCENTI **64**, 38, 74, 85, 98

P
PALAZZI
ACCIAIOLI (or DELLA CERTOSA) **52**
ALBIZI **100**
ANTELLA **149**
ANTINORI **84**
ARTE DEI BECCAI **49**
ARTE DELLA LANA **202**, 52
BARDI **71**
BARTOLINI-SALIMBENI **108**
BORGHESE **182**
BORSA **185**
CALCAGNINI **184**
CANIGIANI **53**
CAPITANI DI PARTE GUELFA **54**
CAPPONI **170**
CAPPONI DA UZZANO **72**
CAPPONI IN OLTRARNO **124**
CARTELLONI **163**
CASTELLI-MARUCELLI **152**
COCCHI-SERRISTORI **99**
CORSINI AL PARIONE **161**
CORSINI-SERRISTORI **102**
COVONI **151**
DAVANZATI **50**
DE' MOZZI **30**
degli Studi 49
Ducale, see palazzo Vecchio
Farnese 88
FERONI-SPINI **32**, 39
Frescobaldi 39
GIANFIGLIAZZI **33**
GINORI **104**
GIUDICI (OR CASTELLANI) **48**
GIUGNI **130**
GONDI **90**, 72
GRIFONI (OR BUDINI-GATTAI) **123**
GUADAGNI **105**
HORNE **88**
LARDEREL **132**
LENZI-QUARATESI **73**
MEDICI-RICCARDI (PALAZZO DI COSIMO IL VECCHIO) **74**, **158**, 9, 65, 67
Medici-Riccardi, Cappella dei Magi 65
Medici-Riccardi, Galleria 105
MISSIONI **154**
NICCOLINI **122**
NONFINITO **133**
ORLANDINI DEL BECCUTO **159**
PANDOLFINI **107**, 16
PANCIATICHI-XIMENES **101**
PAZZI **82**
PITTI (PALAZZO DI LUCA PITTI) **87**, **148**, 55, 72, 86, 88, 109, 148, 180, 189
PITTI, ROYAL SUITE OF APARTMENTS **189**
PITTI, GALLERIA PALATINA **180**
PITTI, DUCAL PALACE **120**
POPOLO (SEE BARGELLO)
Priori, see palazzo Vecchio
PUCCI **129**
RAMIREZ DI MONTALVO **127**
Ricasoli 64
ROSSELLI-DEL TURCO **106**
RUCELLAI **83**, 55
SALVIATI **128**, 92
SAN CLEMENTE **153**
SCALA-DELLA GHERARDESCA **86**
SERRISTORI **192**
Signoria, see palazzo Vecchio
SPECOLA **174**
STROZZI **89**, 55
STROZZI DEL POETA **150**
STROZZINO **75**
TADDEI **103**
UGUCCIONI **117**
VECCHIO (OR DEI PRIORI) **34**, 116, 21, 27, 35, 39, 41, 42, 44, 50, 77, 88
VIVIANI DELLA ROBBIA **164**
ZUCCARI **131**
PALAZZO AND MUSEO BARDINI **200**, 125
PARK AT THE CASCINE **177**, 134
PIAZZE
BECCARIA **195**
CAVOUR (PIAZZA LIBERTÀ) **196**
D'AZEGLIO **194**
INDIPENDENZA **187**, 122
MULINA (PIAZZA POGGI) **197**
REPUBBLICA **199**
Signoria 21
PIAZZALE MICHELANGELO **198**, 123
Politeama (Municipal Theater) 117
PONTEVECCHIO **47**, 88, 129
PORTICO OF THE CONFRATERNITA DEI SERVITI **113**

Q
Questura 113

R
RAILROAD BUILDINGS **213**
RAILROAD STATION OF SANTA MARIA NOVELLA **212**, 137
REGIONAL HEADQUARTERS OF RAI TV **229**
RESIDENTIAL BUILDING IN PIAZZA SAN JACOPINO **232**
RESIDENTIAL BUILDING IN THE VIA PIAGENTINA **225**
RESIDENTIAL COMPLEX AT MONTERINALDI **222**, 129
ROMAN AMPHITHEATER **5**
ROYAL MANSION AT THE CASCINE **178**

S
SACRISTY OF SANTA TRINITA **63**
SACRISTY OF SANTO SPIRITO **93**
SAGRESTIA NUOVA OF SAN LORENZO **109**, 11
SAGRESTIA VECCHIA OF SAN LORENZO **67**, 12
Sala del Capitolo 46

T
TEATRO COMUNALE, or MUNICIPAL THEATER **186,** 117
Tempio di Marte 12
"TEPIDARIUM" GREENHOUSE **193**
Tobacco Processing and Manufacturing Division 131
Tomba dell'Indiano 134
TORRIGIANI GARDEN **181**
TOWER-HOUSES
ALBERTI **27**
AMIDEI (or DELLA BIGONCIA) **26**, 36

143

CORBIZI (OR DEI DONATI) **24**
Macci 51
MARSILI **25**
VEDOVE (OR DEI GHIBERTI) **23**
TOWERS
  de' Foraboschi 42
  DELLA CASTAGNA **22**
  DELLA PAGLIAZZA **13**
  della Zecca 48
  Maratona (City Stadium) 131
  Valognana 38
Tribuna di Galileo 113
Tribunale 110
TRIUMPHAL ARCH **165**

PETRAIA **138**
POGGIO IMPERIALE **171**
STIBBERT **201**
VILLINO BROGGI **211**

U

UFFIZI **118**, 87, 136
University Department of Architecture 103
University Department of Economics 116

V

VASARI'S CORRIDOR **119**, 50, 111
VIALE DEI COLLI **198**
VICHI HOME AND GALLERY **208**

VILLAS
  BARDINI (OR TORRE DEL GALLO) **203**
  CORSINI AT CASTELLO **162**
  CASTELLO **137**
  Farnesina 83
  FAVARD **183**, 116
  Ginori 122
  I COLLAZZI **110**
  LA FERDINANDA **139**
  Medici at Cafaggiolo 68
  MEDICI AT CAREGGI **79**, 68
  MEDICI AT FIESOLE (OR IL PALAGIO) **80**
  MEDICI AT POGGIO A CAIANO **94**, 71
  Medici at Trebbio 68

Index of names

A
Acciaioli (family) 49
Adimari (family) 35
Alberti, Leon Battista 55, 56, 63, 67, 70, 71, 74, 75
Albertini, Francesco 15
Albizi (family) 35
Alighieri, Dante 27
Alterati (circle of artists) 102
Ammannati, Bartolomeo 14, 77, 84, 88, 89, 90, 91, 92, 94, 105
Andrea del Castagno 57
Andrea del Sarto 79
Ariosto, Ludovico 9
Arnaldi, Alberto 45
Arnolfo di Cambio 27, 28, 41, 42, 43, 44, 51
Arte dei Fabbriceri 51
Arte della Lana 58
Arte della Seta 59
Attavanti, Attavante 15

B
Baccani, Gaetano 109, 115, 116, 120
Baccio d'Agnolo 73, 79, 80, 81, 82, 86, 90
Balatri, Giovan Battista 104
Baldi, Pier Maria 105
Bardini, Stefano 124, 125
Bartolamei, Antonio Maria 101
Bazzani, Cesare 127

Beato Angelico 66
Benci di Cione 38, 47, 53
Benedetto da Maiano 9, 73
Benedettini (order) 27, 28
Boccaccio, Giovanni 41
Bocchi 15
Bonaiuti, Telemaco 117
Bonaparte, Napoleone 80
Bonaparte, Paolina 116
Borghese, principe 116
Borromeo, Carlo 47
Borsook 17
Brancacci, Felice 56
Brunelleschi, Filippo 10, 11, 12, 31, 38, 41, 44, 53, 55, 58, 59, 60, 61, 62, 63, 64, 65, 72, 79, 97
Bruni, Leonardo 12
Buontalenti, Bernardo 14, 77, 86, 87, 89, 90, 91, 93, 94, 95, 100, 101, 102, 112
Burci 16
Burckhardt, Jacob 16

C
Caccini, Giovanni 93, 98
Cacialli, Giuseppe 112
Calabi, Donatella 21
Caldini, Luigi 125
Cambiagi 16
Cambio, Arnolfo di 27, 28, 41, 42, 43, 44, 51
Campiobbesi (family) 124
Canella, Carlo 21

Cappello, Bianca 91
Carmelitani (order) 56
Carmelitani Scalzi (order) 104
Carnielo, Rinaldo 126
Carocci 16
Castellucci, Giuseppe 125
Cavalieri di Malta, Sovrano Order dei 34, 78
Cecchini, Alessandro 112
Cerutti, Giulio 104
Cigoli (Ludovico Cardi also known as) 93
Cinelli 15
Ciocchi, Giovan Filippo 110
Cistercensi (order) 28, 41
Clement VII 14
Confraternita degli Scalzi 79
Cosimo de' Medici 12, 55, 91, 97
Cosimo I 77, 85, 87, 88
Cosimo III de' Medici 107
Cosimo il Vecchio 65, 66, 68, 69, 72
Cronaca (Simone del Pollaiolo also known as) 9, 72, 73, 78, 79, 81, 86

D
Dati, Goro 15
Davanzati (family) 124
Davidsohn 16
De Cambray Digny, Luigi 115
De Fabris, Emilio 117, 121
Dei, Benedetto 12, 15

Index of names

De Miranda, Fabrizio 134
Del Moro, Luigi 121
Detti, Edoardo 129, 132, 135
Dezzi Bardeschi, Marco 18, 137
Dini (family) 83
Domenicani (order) 27, 67, 104
Domenicani dell'Osservanza (order) 66
Domenico d'Agnolo, 90
Donatello 12, 61, 97
Donati (family) 35
Dori, Alessandro 113
Dosio, Giovanni Antonio 90, 93
Duca di Atene 37

E
Eleonora di Toledo 88
Enlart 16

F
Fagnoni, Raffaello 18
Falcini, Mariano 121
Fallani, Bernardo 112
Fancelli, Giovanni 49
Fancelli, Luca 72
Fanelli, Giovanni 18
Ferdinando I 77, 94
Ferri, Antonio Maria 10, 97, 104, 105, 106, 107
Foggini, Giovan Battista 97, 98, 105, 107, 111
Fontana, Carlo 112
Fortini, Gaetano 124
Fortini, Gioacchino 110
Francescani (order) 27
Francesco I 77, 91
François 16
Frosali, N. 123

G
Galilei, Galileo 107
Gamberini, Italo 129, 130, 132, 136
Gargiolli 16
Gelati, Lorenzo 20
Gerini, marchese 19
Gesuiti (order) 105
Ghiberti, Lorenzo 31, 35, 58, 59

Giotto 41, 43, 45, 97
Giovannetti, B. 19
Giovanni Battista del Tasso 86
Giovanni da Gaiole 62
Giovanni di Lapo Ghini 44
Giovanni Francesco 82
Giudici di Ruota 50
Giuliano da Maiano 63, 67, 69, 70
Gizdulich, Riccardo 132
Goethe, Johann Wolfgang 16
Gondi, Leonardo 73
Goldthwaite, Richard A. 18
Gonzaga, Ludovico 67
Gozzoli, Benozzo 65
Gregorio X 37
Grote 17

H
Horne, Herbert 72
Horner 16

I
Ildebrando 30

J
Jadot, Jean Nicholas 110

L
Le Corbusier 49
Leonardo da Vinci 86
Leo X 14, 82, 83
Leopoldo II 115
Lippi, Filippo 56
Lorena (family) 87, 109, 120
Lorena, Francesco Stefano di 110
Lorenzo di Bicci 64
Lorenzo il Magnifico 12, 14, 55, 68, 73, 75, 77, 83
Luigi XIV 107
Lupi, Bonifacio 113
Lusini, Enrico 124

M
Magliabechi (Fondo) 127
Majorfi, Michelangelo 117
Malfatti Raimondi, Livia 112
Manetti, Giuseppe 62, 63, 67, 109, 114
Marcellini, Carlo 111
Marenigh 16

Maria Antonia, principessa 117
Martelli, Giuseppe 113
Martucci, R. 19
Marucelli, Francesco 113
Masaccio 56
Masolino 56
Matas, Nicola 120
Mazzoni, Angiolo 18, 130
Medici (family) 11, 14, 60, 68, 72, 82, 83, 94, 97, 109
Medici, Alessandro 84
Medici, Giovanni 100
Mengoni, Giuseppe 120
Michelangelo Buonarroti 14, 77, 83, 84, 86, 94, 123
Michelazzi, Giovanni 119, 126, 127
Micheli, Vincenzo 123, 127
Michelozzo 9, 55, 63, 64, 65, 66, 67, 68, 69, 72, 73, 100
Michelucci, Giovanni 18, 129, 130, 132, 133
Montemagni, Adriano 134
Morandi, Riccardo 132

N
Nelli, Giovan Battista 107
Neri di Fioravante 38, 47, 50
Nervi, Pier Luigi 129, 131
Nigetti, Matteo 97, 98, 99, 100

P
Pandolfini, Giannozzo 82
Paoletti, Gaspare Maria 112
Parigi il Giovane, Alfonso 87, 89, 105
Parigi, Giulio 101, 102, 112
Passavanti, Jacopo 49
Pazzi, Andrea 63
Peruzzi, Baldassarre 83
Petrarca, Francesco 41
Pettirossi, Bartolomeo 99
Pietro da Cortona 106, 110
Pietro del Massaio 9
Pietro Leopoldo 114
Pisano, Andrea 44, 45, 48
Pitti (family) 77
Pitti, Luca 72, 88
Poccianti, Pasquale 109, 112
Poggi, Giuseppe 18, 73, 116,

146